Further Praise for ~~Y~~ Retirement Sm~~i~~

Tim and Mart opened my eyes to how the financial ~~.....~~ *As a practicing orthodontist, I was extremely proficient in my field but woefully ignorant when it came to my finances. The team at Macro Wealth Management has leveled the playing field, giving doctors the tools they need to build wealth.*

—Dr. Tom Shannon, Grandville, MI

A number of years ago, I was invited to attend a "retirement planning lecture." I only attended to not offend my friend. When I returned home that night, I told my wife, "I'm not sure, but I think I just listened to something that will completely change our life in retirement. I was blown away." Since that time, I have worked with Macro Wealth Management and I no longer worry about what my income level will be once I retire. With their strategies—that are not your cookie-cutter, in-the-box, standard ways—I know I will be able to count on my guaranteed income level in retirement.

—Dr. Bill Dischinger, Lake Oswego, OR
key opinion leader, Ormco Corporation

Mart and Tim's data-driven approach to financial "treatment" planning is as intelligent as it is important for us all to hear. I wish I would have heard this information a long time ago!

—Dr. Jamie Reynolds, Novi, MI
~~lea~~der of OrthoFi

Mart and Tim have been instrumental in helping my family to be on the road to achieving our financial goals. From the very beginning, they have taken a "macro" approach to ensure that not only are we investing our money wisely but that we have systems in place to ensure that our family will have financial stability in the event of any unforeseen circumstances. This is not the sale of a "get rich quick" system or a magical "product," instead, this is a careful approach that truly is tailored to help you achieve and maintain financial success!

—Todd Erdman, Wheeling, IL
dental attorney

Mart and Tim are helping investors in general and dentists in particular live the life of their dreams in retirement. They debunk much of the conventional "wisdom" of high-cost, transaction-hungry Wall Street firms and focus on the benefits of planning and discipline. They are consummate professionals in a world often dominated by salespeople.

—Patrick Sweeny, Glastonbury, CT
principal and cofounder, Symmetry Partners, LLC

After powering through the Tony Robbins book, I think Your Retirement Smile *is a much more understandable read!*

—Dr. John Foley, NC

Mart and Tim have sculpted a tremendous pathway to understanding your retirement and a direct line to confidence about your future.

—John Pobanz, South Ogden, UT
clinical professor at the University of Nevada Dental School

Nothing short of masterfully awesome!

—Dr. David Allen, Wheaton, IL

I was a marketing and sales professional in the insurance industry for forty-five years, but even that did not prevent me from making some very poor financial decisions.

While serving as the regional VP for a Midwest-based life insurance company, I met Tim and Mart. Over the course of a few years, Tim and I formed a personal friendship in addition to a very strong business relationship. I finally asked Tim to show me his "process" and, from that encounter, my wife and I became his clients and are we ever glad we did ... our only regret is that we didn't meet Tim earlier! Working with Tim, we are VERY well-positioned in our retirement. I have encouraged both of my sons to seek out Tim and pay heed to his extremely valuable advice.

—Robert Ley, IL

From the very start of my career, I knew regardless of what anyone told me, I wanted to live at the same financial level through my retirement years as I would through my work years. I didn't know how I was going to achieve this goal until I sat down for a meeting with Mart and Tim, friends I've known for years. Macro Wealth Management has enabled me to achieve this goal. This company practices what they preach, and they truly care for their clients. As I sat with Mart and Tim, I did not see salesmen, I saw genuine men who wanted to help me. It has been a pleasure working with them through the years, and I know I can always count on them.

—Dr. Rob Girgis, Woodridge, IL
former president of the Illinois Society of Orthodontists

I have worked with Tim for over fifteen years. In the process of those fifteen years, I have leaned on Tim to assist in every financial decision I have made. From buying vacation property in Park City, Utah, to buying my family business, to making additions to our home and, for sure, building my own strip center for my business twelve years ago, Tim has been there every step of the way. What makes his Treatment Plan different from every other advisor I have worked with in my twenty-plus years of working is the fact that it challenges you to enjoy your life and your earnings now while you are young all the while creating the possibility of living a full-bodied life once you retire. Tim and his Treatment Plan have allowed me to sleep soundly knowing that my family will truly enjoy our best years now, all the while celebrating our golden years with more protection and security than we ever dreamed of. Tim has made my life and my family's life better because of our financial security, and it all goes back to that model that is proven, tested, and solid. Every family should be built on a strong foundation ... our financial future is for sure sound. Thanks, Tim!

—Robert Woolsey, Peoria, IL
president of Jones Bros. Jewelers

Your Retirement Smile *is a refreshing new look on what truly matters regarding retirement planning. It is uniquely and creatively written with new financial ideas and substance. It is not laden with lots of investment or product hype. It zeros in on many facets of financial life, which many financial planners and financial institutions do not consider or disregard. If your current planning makes you feel like you are doing all the right things, but you don't seem to be getting ahead, this book is a must-read. Once you start reading this book, you will not want to put it down. Each page is filled with life-changing ideas for a better and more reassuring financial life. Enjoy!*

—Lenny Martin, CLU, ChFC, RHU

Mart McClellan, DDS, MS, is an expert at creating beautiful and lasting smiles! Now, he has teamed up with Mr. Tim Streid, CLU, to help create lasting smiles for dental professionals into their retirement years. Their combined financial expertise and knowledge of the unique financial position of dental professionals has led to the creation of an invaluable Financial Treatment Plan for retirement. As consultants in the dental field, we know that dental school rarely sets new doctors up for financial and business success. It is a missing part of the curriculum that most doctors desperately need. Through the implementation of evidence-based processes, a macro-economic foundation, and sound financial coaching, doctors following their Financial Treatment Plan can set themselves up for ultimate financial stability in retirement. This information is not only invaluable for dental professionals but for anyone seeking to maximize their financial security in retirement. This is a resource that we will undoubtedly share with every client that we work with!

—Manon Newell, MD
COO Systemized Orthodontics Consulting Group

YOUR
retirement
SMILE

DR. MART McCLELLAN   TIM STREID

YOUR

retirement

SMILE

THE TREATMENT PLAN FOR
PAY-CUT PREVENTION
IN YOUR GOLDEN YEARS

Advantage®

Published by Advantage, Charleston, South Carolina.
Member of Advantage Media Group.

ADVANTAGE is a registered trademark, and the Advantage colophon is a trademark of Advantage Media Group, Inc.

Printed in the United States of America.

10 9 8 7 6 5 4 3 2 1

ISBN: 978-1-59932-956-7
LCCN: 2019911008

Book design by Jamie Wise.

This publication is designed to provide accurate and authoritative information in regard to the subject matter covered. It is sold with the understanding that the publisher is not engaged in rendering legal, accounting, or other professional services. If legal advice or other expert assistance is required, the services of a competent professional person should be sought.

Advantage Media Group is proud to be a part of the Tree Neutral® program. Tree Neutral offsets the number of trees consumed in the production and printing of this book by taking proactive steps such as planting trees in direct proportion to the number of trees used to print books. To learn more about Tree Neutral, please visit www.treeneutral.com.

Advantage Media Group is a publisher of business, self-improvement, and professional development books and online learning. We help entrepreneurs, business leaders, and professionals share their Stories, Passion, and Knowledge to help others Learn & Grow. Do you have a manuscript or book idea that you would like us to consider for publishing? Please visit advantagefamily.com or call 1.866.775.1696.

We would like to dedicate this book to our wives, Lindsey and Julie, who have been there every step of the way. They held down the fort and cared for our children while we were away, lecturing across the country, attending meetings, or meeting with clients—assistance that was invaluable to our success. We could not have done it without you! Although our children weren't always aware of the help we were providing to our clients, we thank them for their hugs, kisses, and smiles when we returned home from our trips and their support through the years. We would also like to acknowledge all of our clients who have embraced our information. They have seen firsthand that there is a much better way to create incredible life enjoyment for themselves and their families. It is a magical moment when our clients first realize they can retire on their terms with much more income, more guarantees, less risk, and no additional out-of-pocket outlay. This cannot be done in the traditional world of personal finance, which is why we have written this book.

CONTENTS

• • •

Introduction *1*

NOBODY LIKES A PAY CUT

Chapter 1 . . . . *15*

THE FIGHT FOR YOUR MONEY

Chapter 2 . . . . *35*

THE BIG MONEY PICTURE

Chapter 3 . . . . *59*

EVEN THE LONE RANGER HAD TONTO

Chapter 4 . . . . *71*

MONEY MYTHS DEBUNKED

Chapter 5 . . . . *109*

PUTTING YOUR MONEY IN POSITION

Chapter 6 . . . . *125*

LANDING YOUR MONEY SAFELY

Chapter 7 . . . . *145*

IS YOUR RETIREMENT INCOME A SURE THING?

Chapter 8 . . . . *161*

MAKING YOUR GOLDEN
YEARS GOLDEN

Conclusion *173*

THE FINANCIAL ENJOYMENT FACTOR

Acknowledgments 183

About Macro Wealth Management 185

Introduction

NOBODY LIKES
A PAY CUT

• • •

*As you walk down the fairway of life, you must smell
the roses, for you only get to play one round.*

—BEN HOGAN

It is safe to say that no one likes to take a pay cut—*ever*. Yet, almost every American and dentist will take one in retirement! For many, it will be a big pay cut. This is why the information in this book is so important for you, your family, and the charities to which you want to contribute. You are about to embark on a financial journey that will change how you approach your financial decision making. If you can remain open minded, your financial life will forever be transformed.

Our objective is to put a smile on your face when it comes to retirement and remove the trepidations (or frowns) that so many have when they enter their golden years. It will likely make you feel a bit uncomfortable at times. Why? Because almost everything you have been told about being financially successful is a half truth or misinformation. It will be frustrating because you will ask yourself many times, *Why haven't I been told this in the past?* or think to yourself, *I thought there might be a better way.* The good news is that it is not too late to implement these strategies and become significantly wealthier, have more free time to spend with your family and friends, and have the ability to make a great contribution to society through charitable giving!

Since time is a limited resource, it is an extremely valuable asset. Hence, having more free time is what everyone wants. In her book, *The Top Five Regrets of the Dying,* Australian nurse Bronnie Ward writes that one of the regrets shared among those who are dying is that they wish they hadn't worked so hard. In her research, family and relationship expert Hellen Chen found that "the deepest regret that I have heard has been men and women missing out on the most important part of life: the quality of their relationship in a marriage and/or with their children." The beauty of the information within this book is that it creates so much security now and retirement income for the future that it expands time, giving people more time for the important things in their lives.

Pick up any magazine article on money, listen to the financial gurus or entertainers on the radio or television, or read financial advice online and you will believe that people fall into two groups when it comes to money: savers and spenders, with spenders having a more negative connotation.

The truth is money is not an either/or thing. It is not now *or* later. It is not all *or* nothing. When it comes to your money, you *can* have your cake and eat it too. You can save *and* spend. You can invest for the future *and* enjoy your life in the present. You can enjoy life to its fullest during your working years and have 100 percent income replacement when you retire. How? By following a macroeconomic financial process that allows you to enjoy your life now *and* retire without taking a pay cut or having the fear of running out of money. This is how we create your retirement smile!

In the dental world, the 2010 report on retirement, published by the American Dental Association (ADA), shows that dentists take, on average, a 50 percent pay cut the moment they retire. When we meet dentists across the country, we find this number to be about right. Think of this in terms dentists know well: taking a test. If you are studying to become a dentist and you get a 50 percent grade, you are failing. It is unacceptable. So, if you retire with a 50 percent drop in income, didn't your financial plan just fail? The answer is a resounding yes, yet that is the path most dentists and Americans will be on until they read this book.

No dentist wants to fail or struggle when it comes to their personal finances. The acceptance of anything less than full income replacement in retirement is less than successful. Oftentimes, traditional financial advisors[1] will justify the reduced income, such as 70 percent of your preretirement income, by saying that is all you need, but is that what you want? If you could position yourself to retire with full income replacement, at no additional out-of-pocket cost to you, wouldn't you want that? Instead of receiving a failing grade in personal finance you would receive an A+. Who would you rather be: the stellar financial student with minimal worries in retirement or the one who does what everyone else is doing and in retirement has less income, more risk, and increased stress?

Individuals make financial decisions every day, whether it is buying a car or house, paying off student loans or consumer debt, paying for a child's college expenses, purchasing an insurance product,

---

1   We will reference traditional advisors many times in this book. These advisors include certified financial planners, nationwide dental advisory firms, online forums and blogs, radio personalities, financial magazines, stockbrokers, accountants, lawyers, and life insurance agents.

saving for retirement, or making various investment decisions, just to name a few. Each of these decisions is made at specific points in our lifetime with different advisors, who usually have differing opinions. We call these decisions *microeconomic* decisions. The truth is, however, a benign decision, such as how you pay your mortgage, not only affects the mortgage on your house (micro), but it also affects many other aspects of your financial life from a *macroeconomic* perspective. It is essential to understand this interaction, something that will be explained later in the book.

The big question is, How do you know what is right? If you are making every financial decision from a microeconomic viewpoint only, then by default, you lose the added benefits and value that a macroeconomic approach to your financial decision making brings to the table. Ignoring the macroeconomic impact of a financial decision causes individuals to unknowingly lose hundreds of thousands of dollars, if not millions, over their lifetime. This is why most dentists are only retiring on half of their preretirement income.

Purchasing financial products in the wrong way will not only cost you a ton of money, but the misunderstood strategies that are sold with these products will prove to be even more costly today and in retirement. Touted traditional financial strategies, such as the compounding of interest in a taxable environment, excessive tax deferrals for retirement plan contributions, or the acceleration of debt repayment, are just a few of the many weak recommendations made by advisors across the country. Each of them will contribute to a disappointing retirement from an income standpoint. Wrong products with the wrong strategies create a significant pay cut in retirement.

Reading this book for the first time may make you feel uncomfortable. Your unease will be due to the fact that you will recognize many of these traditional strategies as ones that you are presently employing in your current financial plan. One of the many purposes of this book is to help you discover, through an evidence-based process, why these strategies are weak. At the same time, you will be introduced to a comprehensive process and framework for evaluating financial decisions from an economic basis that will allow a paradigm shift and make your financial life significantly better.

Most dentists we work with enjoy their profession, but as much as they do, it is safe to say they will retire at some point. It is not a matter of *if* you will retire as much as it is *what kind* of retirement you will have: a very fruitful retirement, or one that only has some fruit on the retirement tree. An abundant, fruitful tree enables you to continue working because you want to and not because you have to.

The hard facts are that only 5 percent of dentists can retire comfortably.[2] This is a shocking number. The vast majority of dentists have no idea that their present situations can be so much better. One question you should ask yourself is, If all the financial information promoted by traditional advisors, the media, online forums and blogs, financial institutions, corporations, and our parents/friends/colleagues is so good, why aren't more dentists able to retire successfully? Also, why are seniors running out of money in retirement? The answer is that they don't have a strategic, macro-Financial Treatment Plan. This book is the Financial Treatment Plan for pay-cut prevention in your golden years!

---

2   "2010 Survey on Retirement and Investment," American Dental Association, https://ebusiness.ada.org/productcatalog/452/Dentistry/2010-Survey-on-Retirement-and-Investment-Downloadable-SC/SRI-2010D#.

Mart

I'm from a middle-class family that has their roots in the Midwest. My father was the first to graduate from college. As a young child, I was raised in West Virginia and then, as a teenager, I moved to Connecticut. I was recruited to play golf and basketball at DePauw University, where I went on two mission trips to Kenya and Guatemala and discovered dentistry. My interest in dentistry led me to Northwestern University Dental School and, finally, to the University of Michigan orthodontic residency program.

Like most Americans, financial planning was never a significant topic of conversation for the first thirty years of my life, other than my grandparents talking about saving money because they only had pea soup to eat during the Depression years! After graduating from my orthodontic residency with a ton of student loan debt, my wife and I engaged some financial advisors, who gave traditional advice. I thought they were doing the right things with our money until one day, after an annual review, our advisor recommended that we switch from one product we bought from him years before to another product. We thought that what we had purchased years before was appropriate, but now it was not? It did not seem or smell right, but how were we to know?

Maybe it was divine intervention, but just as I was about to finalize that decision with my traditional advisor, I met Tim. I didn't know Tim from Adam. He was advising one of my dental school classmates who said Tim had helped him out a lot. When we first met, Tim said he could actually measure financial decisions with a macro-economic system he used and verify what option would give me greater output from a rate of return and benefits standpoint. I asked him if he could take the product my wife and I had bought three years earlier and compare it to the change our advisor was now recommending. At that point Tim had no skin in the game other than showing me his powerful system.

Tim showed me clearly, with a side-by-side comparison, that what we had purchased years before was the more appropriate path for us. The new recommendation was nothing more than a way for our old advisor to churn the account for a commission. That single decision to keep in place what my wife and I had originally purchased changed our financial life forever. It also allowed us to do things we would not have been able to do if we had made that switch. From that point, we were Tim's clients for the next seven years.

● ● ● ● ● ● ● ● ● ● ● ● ● ● ● ● ● ●

● ● ● ● ● ● ● ● ● ● ● ● ● ● ● ● ● ●

Tim

During the time I advised Mart and Lindsey, the stock market crashed after the dot-com era and the September 11 terror attack on the twin towers. Despite this, Mart's financial life was thriving. On the other hand, many of

Mart's friends' and colleagues' financial situations were not as good, due to the volatile stock market. It was at that time that Mart and I made the decision to share our information with the dental community. We started doing some speaking engagements together and writing joint articles in national publications. Our message started gaining some traction, and we had the opportunity to lecture both nationally and internationally.

That's when we decided to take things to the next level and start our advisory firm, Macro Wealth Management, in 2004. It's hard to believe it's been fifteen years now.

● ● ● ● ● ● ● ● ● ● ● ● ● ● ● ● ● ●

Our Financial Treatment Plan is based on the theories of economist Robert Castiglione, who developed his model in 1980. The most powerful part of his system is that it has stood the test of time through good and bad markets and ever-changing tax laws and interest rate environments. Successful planning comes from plans that work under even the worst-case scenario, and this is what Bob Castiglione created. It would be safe to say that anything better than a worst-case scenario is fantastic!

With backgrounds in financial planning and dentistry, which is our unique value proposition, we established Macro Wealth Management, using a comprehensive financial model as the foundation for our advisory practice. Because of our unique backgrounds, the lion's share of our work is done in the dental profession, but the concepts work for everyone.

Dental school offers very little, if any, training in personal finance or practice management. When you graduate from dental school, you are Little Red Riding Hood, and the financial advisor is the wolf dressed as Grandma. The wolf thinks you have or will have a lot of money due to the word *doctor* being part of your title. The truth is you may have as much as half a million dollars in student loan debt and no money to buy a home or a practice.

This is the typical plight of a new dental graduate. As a new dentist, you have no idea how to start a practice or run a business, let alone how to deal with your personal finances. Your focus becomes being a good dentist, which is fantastic, but this comes at the expense of personal wealth building.

Because you are so focused on building your business, you begin to lose sight of the personal financial management side of the equation. Instead, you hire a financial advisor or certified financial planner, whose primary focus is selling products or developing plans that are linear in fashion. You buy in, pay the significant fees, and get a financial plan in a three-ring binder that is mostly boilerplate.

That three-ring binder pretty much just sits on your shelf and collects dust. Implementation of the plan, which is essential for success, may not even occur, as the planning fee has already been paid. If a product is purchased, it is often done in a very ineffective manner with no coordination or integration of the product in the overall Financial Treatment Plan. Time goes by and you meet with your advisor here and there. Then, three years later the stock market is going crazy and your advisor wants to get together. Your advisor says you need to replace what you bought three years earlier because the stock market is now booming and you don't want to miss out. This tactic is known as the weak FOMO (fear of missing out) strategy. If you move to the new investment at this time, however, you will buy into a rising market, which is the opposite of what you should be doing. Confronted with this situation, you don't know what is right, nor do you have the time to research it, so you buy again. This is the normal cycle of financial distress in which most dentists find themselves.

Many dentists who are approaching retirement today, or are actually retired, are leading what we refer to as quiet lives of economic desperation. They may look good on the outside, but when you look at their personal finances, it is obvious that they are struggling or distressed due to the enormous uncertainty of the future.

The struggle or stress that the vast majority of dentists experience is resolved when a holistic Financial Treatment Plan is introduced into their lives. It is not just about looking at a retirement plan or investments. It is also about analyzing hard assets, such as real estate, your dental practice, gold, silver, cryptocurrencies such as Bitcoin, artwork, and so on. Your liquidity also plays a significant role in the equation, as does how you are protected with your auto, homeowners, and liability insurance coverage. It also takes into consideration your disability and life insurance, your wills and trust, and your debt situation. *Every* decision you make within that Financial Treatment Plan will always impact something else within the plan. If you don't have a framework from which to measure financial decisions, then you won't know where the problems or inefficiencies exist. They will go unseen. A Financial Treatment Plan provides a macroeconomic picture of your financial life. Its presence is the underlying factor that allows you to achieve a successful retirement versus one that is mediocre at best.

Many dentists head into retirement knowing they are in trouble, but not wanting to admit it. Other dentists think they are totally fine because they have accumulated a lot of money. However, many of these dentists are also in trouble if they don't have a distribution plan in place for their income. No matter how much money you have, without an efficient distribution plan in place, you are still going to take a pay cut in retirement or not live life to its fullest. Even if you have been extremely successful and have done all the right things from a traditional financial standpoint, you will still not be doing as well as you could be doing because the track you are on is not efficient.

It does not have to be that way.

Dentists make a great income, which is certainly above the income of the average American household. The problem for dentists is not that they don't make enough money. They make plenty of money. The problem is that their money is not positioned appropriately.

Whether we make $50,000 a year or $500,000 a year, we all have a finite amount of money that will enter our lives during our lifetime. Every dollar that comes in is precious. We have to understand how money works and how to best make money work for us. With that being said, each dollar has a specific position at a particular time for ultimate efficiency. The question you should ask yourself is, Am I confident that my money is positioned perfectly for maximum output to ensure more benefits and multiple income streams in retirement?

Most dentists believe that a successful retirement is based solely on how big their pile of assets is at retirement. There is actually a book published in the world of personal finance that asks, "What's your number?" for retirement, as if that has anything to do with a successful retirement.[3] According to a *Journal of Clinical Orthodontics* survey, respondents felt that $2,000,000 was the threshold for being ready for retirement.[4] What is your number or how big does your

---

3   Lee Eisenberg, *The Number: A Completely Different Way to Think About the Rest of Your Life (New York: Free Press, 2006).*

4   Jeremiah Sturgill and Jae Park, "Changes in Orthodontists' Retirement Planning and Practice Operations Due to the Recent Recession," *Journal of Clinical Orthodontics* 49, no. 4 (April 2015): 240–8.

pile of assets have to be for you to achieve the retirement of your dreams? Would $10,000,000 be enough? Would you be content with that number?

Most dentists would be extremely happy to be in that position, but let's not forget that life is relative. It is safe to say that if you are a dentist with that much money saved for retirement, your income was probably upward of $500,000 a year for the better part of your career, maybe closer to over $1 million a year.

Let's assume you were earning $500,000 a year in your practice, before retirement. In the traditional world of financial planning, the $10,000,000 of retirement assets will deliver $300,000 of retirement income using a 3 percent safe withdrawal strategy (explained later). Now, $300,000 is a lot of money, but you were making a half million dollars before you retired. That means you will have a huge 40 percent pay cut in retirement! Some may think that $300,000 in retirement is more than enough income, but if you could have more, would that be a better result?

Our view is that if you were to position your money correctly and use the *same* dollars (we're not saying put more money in; we're saying use the same dollars to do more), your retirement income could be $500,000 or more, as opposed to $300,000. That's right. Simply by reworking the money in your Financial Treatment Plan, substantially more retirement income is possible. Why wouldn't you want that?

If you were to take a 50 percent pay cut in retirement, regardless of your previous income, the lifestyle you were accustomed to while engaged in your career would be reduced significantly in your golden years. Therein lies the problem, because no matter what income level you achieve, it is impossible to live the same lifestyle on half of the money. This problem would be further compounded if no guarantees were built in to your plan. Hence, having more retirement income resolves this problem whether you are a spender or a saver!

Think about the opportunities you would have if you had full income replacement in retirement that was inflation protected. One, your lifestyle would not change. Two, if you didn't feel you needed or wanted the additional dollars, you could invest them back into your Financial Treatment Plan and leave a larger legacy for loved ones and charities. These dollars could be used to spoil grandkids or pay for their college educations. You could take your family on vacations beyond their wildest dreams. If you were to have $200,000 in annual income that you don't need, you could donate it to a charity or to a cause you are passionate about. With full income replacement in retirement, you have the opportunity to do all of these things because you *want* to do them. That extra income would give you security, options, and flexibility that would not be possible with less income. Most importantly, you would have the greatest gift of all: financial peace of mind.

Almost all the financial information that we are exposed to from the many different outlets soliciting us is misinformation. It is voluminous. This doesn't mean it is *totally* wrong. It may be right from a *micro* standpoint, but it is wrong from a *macro* standpoint. When it is wrong from a macroeconomic standpoint, your resulting income and enjoyment will be less. This is the suboptimal nature of conventional wisdom!

This concept of micro versus macro is also true for those dentists who decide to manage their own finances or follow the path of their successful parents. Managing your financial future in this way is a guarantee of less income, something that most people do not want. As successful as some of our parents are, the concept of income replacement in retirement is something most have never discussed and they, too, may be taking a pay cut in their golden years! This will be discussed in more detail in chapter 3.

We have yet to come across a single instance where our Financial Treatment Plan did not provide more retirement income and benefits. When a dentist uses a macroeconomic system to analyze and verify each financial decision, a financially successful retirement can be accomplished. This is evidence-based planning at its best.

Our hope is that everyone who reads this book discovers a new mind-set when it comes to making financial decisions. We want you to recognize that the same-old-same-old or cookie-cutter approach to finances does not have to be accepted, nor should it be. Also, we want you to have the curiosity and the desire to seek out a different life when it comes to retirement. But we don't want you to just read this book. Instead, we want you to take action and find a better way to make your money work for you and your family as you go forward.

Your mind-set will certainly have to change because as you read the following pages, you will realize that what you are presently doing will not get you to full income replacement in retirement. The following material has stood the test of time in different economic environments and will encourage a paradigm shift. This information will not only have a significant impact on you and your family but also on society if you have a charitable intent.

Chapter 1

THE FIGHT FOR YOUR MONEY

• • •

All wealth is a product of knowledge.

—GEORGE GILDER

When building or creating wealth, there are two prevailing economic principles of money that can be followed: accumulation and acceleration. The accumulation principle focuses on simple math and ways to accumulate and compound your wealth over time. The acceleration principle emphasizes achieving exponential growth through strategies that allow more than one use for every dollar and each use of your dollar creates a new rate of return with additional benefits. In essence, the acceleration principle keeps your money in motion and accelerates your wealth over time. Which principle do you follow: accumulation or acceleration?

Where do these principles originate and which are the entities that decide the rules in the world of finance? There are actually three: the government, financial institutions, and corporations. We refer to these three entities as the rainmakers. A viable, capitalistic society requires the presence of all three entities. We would not want to live in a society where any one of these entities did not exist.

Let's look at a situation in which all three of these entities are intertwined within our economy. The government exists and thrives on a large and continuing tax revenue base. In an effort to spur the economy, the government may create tax breaks or credits for real estate developers and investors to build low-income housing for the poor. This, in turn, puts people to work and creates revenue and profits for the developer and all the subcontractors and suppliers employed in the real estate project. Corporations and businesses further benefit from the new construction as individual homeowners seek to buy furnishings and appliances for their new home. Financial institutions also benefit from the new mortgages and various insurance coverage acquired and purchased by the new homeowners.

The scenario just described creates a win-win-win situation for all three of the rainmakers. The initial tax benefit offered by the government should increase profits generated by corporations and financial institutions and drive tax revenues. Also, when people are employed, the income and payroll tax base is maintained or increases with a growing and productive economy. Corporations and businesses, including their individual shareholders and owners, are happy with the increased sales revenues and business profits. Finally, financial institutions continue to count their money due to the interest and fees generated from the new loans and insurance premiums they collect. As shown, all three of the rainmakers can work together to create and support a vibrant economy.

With this in mind, however, let's not lose sight of the rainmakers' ultimate objective, which is to take and control of as much of our money as possible. Although we are in a fight with the rainmakers for our money, we don't have to live by the rules they create for consumers. Their rules are designed to put money in their coffers and not ours. The rules they live by *accelerate* wealth, which is the exact opposite of what they tell consumers (you and me) to do: *accumulate* wealth. Hence, the money rains and flows into their accounts while it drips or dribbles into ours. Thus, the fight for our money is ongoing, every day of our lives.

RAINMAKER INTERACTION

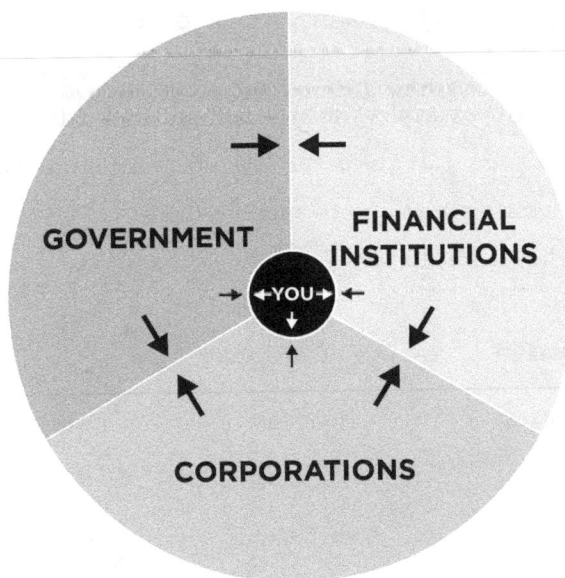

Figure 1.1

- Finite resources in our world
- The three rainmakers are constantly fighting for our money
- Rules change. Laws and new products are created to get more of our money

Today, most dentists who want to build wealth are unknowingly following the path of accumulating and compounding rather than accelerating their money. To find dentists who are accelerating their money is as rare as seeing an albino alligator. The three rainmakers, however, follow the wealth-building acceleration principle by keeping their money in motion. Again, they do the exact opposite of what they advise you and me to do. This is what drives their success and why they have the biggest and tallest buildings in every city across America.

The rainmakers are very skilled at separating you and me from our money. They employ many tactics to do this and frequently accomplish it without their actions being given a second thought by consumers. For example, the government uses different forms of taxation (see Figure 1.2) from the federal, state, and local level to reduce or influence our ability to succeed financially. An IRS auditor once said, "The trick is to stop thinking of it as 'your' money."

GOVERNMENT	CORPORATIONS	FINANCIAL INSTITUTIONS
Federal Taxes	Inflation	Investment Fees
State Taxes	Technological Change	Advisor Fees
Local Taxes	Style Changes	Inefficient Advice
Real Estate Taxes	Planned Obsolescence	Loan Interest
Sales Taxes	Advertising	Commissions
Capital Gains Taxes	False Advertising	Premiums
Estate Taxes	Quality Shrinkage	Market Losses
Licensing Fees	Quantity Shrinkage	Market Volatility
Gov't Student Loans	Service & Repair Fees	Penalties

Ways That the Rainmakers Take Our Money

Figure 1.2

Financial institutions grab our money through fees, commissions, bad advice, and scams. Corporations produce products with built-in planned obsolescence, requiring them to be replaced sooner than should be necessary, or they simply tweak the technology of an existing product and promote the new product as something you can't live without. The ongoing unveiling of the newest smartphone is a great example of this.

Finally, an underlying result of the rainmakers' quest for our money is the introduction of inflation into our lives. Inflation is a stealth tax that erodes a huge amount of our wealth over our lifetime. Many times, the impact of inflation is not fully understood until the consumer is in retirement and on a fixed income.

● ● ● ● ● ●

Inflation is when you pay fifteen dollars for the ten-dollar haircut you used to get for five dollars when you had hair.

—SAM EWING

● ● ● ● ● ●

All rainmakers have their own, individual game plan. The government is starving for taxes that keep it running. Corporations are hungry to sell products to satisfy shareholders. Financial institutions are fighting for the control of large blocks of our money, whether it is in the form of bank deposits, investments, or the sale of insurance products. These deposits all generate massive income in fees for the financial institutions. Yet, there are also times when the rainmakers work together.

A retirement plan is a perfect example of how financial institutions and the government work together to control huge monetary assets. First, the financial institution creates the mind-set that you must have a retirement account if you are ever going to retire, which is actually not true. This is promulgated by the accountants and advisors who share this same belief. As a result, you are convinced to contribute money to a retirement savings plan held at a financial institution.

Typically, the financial institution will get your money on an ongoing basis through weekly or biweekly payroll deductions. Once the financial institution has your money in hand, your money is, essentially, in jail, due to government rules that discourage you from withdrawing these funds prior to the age (as of today) of fifty-nine and a half. This restriction is a huge win for financial institutions as they get to control large blocks of money for a long period of time and collect their fees. If you withdraw your money prior to age fifty-nine and a half you will pay a 10 percent IRS penalty. Therefore, it is very expensive to get that money out of jail before you are fifty-nine and a half. The government is the entity that makes the rules on age of distribution, the type of taxes that need to be paid, penalties, and many other rules.

Now, when you get to retirement age, the rainmakers still want to retain control of your money. At that time, the financial institutions and traditional advisors will tell you that if you withdraw money from your retirement plan you will pay taxes on it, which is true. If you would like to avoid these taxes, though, the financial institutions and traditional advisors have a solution: you can simply defer distributions from this account until age seventy and a half. However, at that point, the government is going to *force* you to start taking withdrawals from your retirement plan through the required minimum distribution (RMD) provision. At this point, the government wants to start collecting on the account holder's deferred tax bill. The adoption of an RMD-only withdrawal strategy for retirement funds allows the financial institutions to hang on to your money and continue to collect ongoing fees for assets under their management.

The worst part of this whole situation is that the owners of the retirement plan end up getting little enjoyment from their retirement assets. The RMD distribution may minimize taxes, but at what expense to the retirees? They are now living on a minimum versus a maximum income distribution, all for the sake of further delaying a tax. Isn't the purpose of funding your retirement plan to fully enjoy it in the future? If so, you should be taking *maximum* distributions out of your retirement plan and not minimum distributions!

●   ●   ●   ●   ●   ●   ●   ●   ●   ●   ●   ●   ●   ●   ●   ●

Tim

I graduated from college in 1984 and went to work for a big-eight public accounting firm. A month after starting, the senior partner called a meeting to introduce us to the new retirement plan that everybody was going to love. It was called a 401(k), which would replace the firm's long-standing defined benefit plan. As some of you may already know, a defined benefit plan is funded 100 percent by the company, which is great for the employee. A 401(k) plan, on the other hand, is, by and large, funded 100 percent by the employee, which is not great. This was the beginning of a huge shift that was taking place in corporations all over America at the time. Pensions were slowly being phased out and replaced by 401(k) plans. This shift was not advantageous to the consumers as they now became largely responsible for the funding of their own retirement.

The 401(k)'s selling point to me was the firm's matching contribution. If I were willing to contribute at least 3 percent, the firm would fully match the 3 percent contribution. With this in mind, right out of the gate, I started contributing 10 percent to the plan. Now in 1984, coming out of school as a certified public accountant, I made a whopping $18,000 a year. What tax bracket do you think I was in at that time? It was 10 percent, or the lowest bracket. It was nothing! Essentially, I deferred the 10 percent tax I would have paid on my money by putting my money into a retirement plan. If I were to retire today, those initial contributions that would otherwise have been taxed at 10 percent would now be taxed at the highest income tax bracket.

So who won that game? It wasn't me. In reality, it was the three rainmakers consisting of the government, corporations, and financial institutions. It's almost as if they colluded with one another at the expense of the consumer—or dentist.

● ● ● ● ● ● ● ● ● ● ● ● ● ● ● ● ● ● ●

401(k)s were promoted to employees as a wonderful retirement option. In reality, the introduction of the 401(k) plan shifted not only the bulk of the funding but also all of the market risk away from the corporations to the individual. Financial institutions were thrilled with the restrictive laws imposed on the 401(k) plans, which prevented individuals from removing funds from their plans prior to age fifty-nine and a half, without incurring an early withdrawal penalty from the IRS. As a result, this one law alone has locked up billions of dollars in invested funds with the financial institutions that are collecting advisory and management fees. The fees collected each year are like a huge annuity to the financial institutions whether the market does well or not.

Finally, those who have a retirement plan such as a 401(k) plan are in a one-sided partnership with the government in that the government makes all of the rules and laws regarding a 401(k) plan. The government tells us how much we can contribute to the plan, at what age we can take funds out of the plan, and how much we will, ultimately, pay in taxes. Also, keep in mind that all long-term capital gains in a retirement plan are taxed as ordinary income and not as capital gains. Tax rates on ordinary income can be as high as 37 percent versus a capital gains rate as low as 15 percent—if the funds were held in an after-tax investment account. For this one fact alone, the difference in potential tax revenues between ordinary and capital gains taxes to the government will be significant over time. We also must take into consideration that tax rates may very well increase over time, which will benefit the government even more. The 401(k) plan and everything that goes along with it is a prime example of how all three rainmakers benefit at the expense of the consumer.

There was a time when you could withdraw your retirement funds at any age, without penalty. Then the government, due to intense lobbying from the financial institutions, put in place restrictive regulations that included penalties for withdrawing money from a retirement account before age fifty-nine and a half. The government can regulate or deregulate, and it can do this in favor or not in favor of the consumer. Therefore, we must be cognizant that laws governing retirement plans can and will change in the future, whether it is for the advantage or disadvantage of the consumer.

If the rainmakers are always moving money under their control for their benefit, then doesn't it make sense that your money should always be in motion too? Anything in life that sits in one place too long will go stale or break down. In other words, it stagnates! Whether it is your health or your money, you need to keep it moving.

Often, dentists resist the concept of money in motion. What they really want is to put their money somewhere and not have to think about it again. They just want to make a money decision and be done with it. Since compound interest is believed to be a good thing in the traditional world of finance, they think they are okay, when in reality their money is rotting right before their eyes.

Why? It's due to the fact that dentists, and the general public, have been directed by financial institutions, accountants, family members, and others to think this way. When we let our money stagnate with the financial institutions, the financial institutions, along with the advisors, are collecting a fee on that invested money. They make money whether your account balance is going up or down. Why would the financial institutions and their many advisors want to give up managing trillions of dollars when they collect a fee that can be 1 percent or higher each and every year?

Over time, dentists will purchase many different insurance and financial products. These purchases are often made one at a time, with different advisors or agents, at different times in a dentist's life. Once the decision about the purchase is made, it is never revisited. This creates a lot disorganization. Everyone knows that disorganization is never good and results in extreme inefficiency when it comes to building wealth. This assortment of unorganized financial products is like your kitchen junk drawer in that you know what is in the drawer, but it takes a while to find what you want.

In this personal financial junk drawer, nothing is coordinated or integrated. Decisions that were made at different points in life are now oftentimes working against each other—very inefficient. This becomes stressful for dentists, but they don't know how to fix it, and so avoid the issue. They don't want to deal with it until introduced to our Financial Treatment Plan.

When you have a Financial Treatment Plan, the disorganization and confusion disappears. Everything is put in its appropriate place and every decision is evaluated from a macroeconomic standpoint. This alone brings tremendous peace of mind to dentists in their personal financial lives. A Financial Treatment Plan allows them to actually visualize and understand their finances and not fear them. It gets them excited to have a better understanding of how their money works and allows them to be proactive with their financial decisions rather than reactive.

When it comes to retirement planning, dentists are taught to max out their retirement contributions but are not taught how to maximize other aspects of their financial lives. If they are only accumulating money, a lot of other people (e.g., financial institutions and advisors) benefit from such a decision without the dentists even knowing it.

That problem is further compounded because there is usually no discussion about an exit or distribution strategy for retirement. Without this discussion, as we said earlier, most retired dentists are leading quiet lives of economic desperation. This is due to the blind focus they placed on only accumulating assets during their working years, with little or no conversation regarding distribution in retirement. They may still be living in the same house and driving the same car (although it is a few years older), but things are tight—and that's just unnecessary.

● ● ● ● ● ● ● ● ● ● ● ● ● ● ● ● ● ● ●

Tim

Various financial magazines will tell you that you only need 60–70 percent of your income in retirement. Better yet, you can have a successful retirement in Costa Rica because the cost of living is so cheap there, or you can move to a US state with no state income tax. The articles will sing the praises of the expat life or living in a state with no state income tax, and they may be right. Your cost of living and taxes may be less as a result of these choices, but you may retire without having family, friends, and everything you know around you. What kind of life is that? That doesn't sound like happiness. Who wants to live out retirement only seeing kids and grandkids once a year? Is that the lasting memory you want to have of them? Living in a foreign country or a tax-free state may be great, if done because you choose to live that way, and not because you have to!

● ● ● ● ● ● ● ● ● ● ● ● ● ● ● ● ● ● ●

We can be angry about the control the rainmakers have over our money, or we can learn from their actions. We have established that financial institutions work on the principle of keeping money in motion, or the velocity of money principle, so let's look at an example. We open a bank account where we make ongoing deposits. Depending on the type of account, the bank may pay us a small amount of interest. Once the bank has our money on deposit, does it just sit on it? The answer is a resounding *no.* The bank will take our money, as well as that of other bank depositors, and use it to its benefit. The bank doesn't sit on the money, as it tells us to do. Instead, it turns around and makes a loan to another individual. Perhaps it's a car loan for one person, and a mortgage loan for somebody else. Then it makes a loan to a college student. As the loan payments come back into the bank, what does the bank do? It lends that money again. The Federal Reserve says that every dollar that moves through a banking institution can turn over as many as fifty-five times each year, or about once a week.[5] But not for you.

Conventional thinking will have you believe that when the bank charges you 4 percent for a car loan and you're earning 1 percent on your savings account at the bank, that bank is only making 3 percent on this transaction. In reality, however, that 3 percent spread represents a 300 percent profit for the bank. As previously discussed, the bank will repeat the transaction, creating new loans with your money many times over during the course of the year. Is it any wonder that banks have some of the largest buildings in every city across the world? This is an example of velocity of money at its finest.

● ● ● ● ● ● ● ● ● ● ● ● ● ● ● ● ● ● ●

Mart

Remember the 1960s television show *The Beverly Hillbillies*? In one episode, Jed Clampett, the millionaire hillbilly, visits Mr. Drysdale, the president of the bank. Jed asks to see his money. He wants Mr. Drysdale to show him his million dollars. Jed was assuming that there was a stack of bills sitting in the bank's vault that was his money. Of course, even then, Jed's money was moving all over the

---

5   Gottfried Leibbrandt, "How fast is that buck?" The SWIFT Institute, July 23, 2012, https://swiftinstitute.org/2012/07/how-fast-is-that-buck.

place. So, Mr. Drysdale ends up showing him a picture of a million dollars just to appease him. Of course, the money pictured wasn't really Jed's money, as banks *do not* let the money sit and stagnate.

• • • • • • • • • • • • • • • • • • • •

Traditionally, if we have money in a bank or an investment account, as it earns interest, dividends, and capital gains, we have been taught to compound the earnings right back into the account. If we do that, we lose control of the asset because we have just allowed those earnings to compound back into the account and go stale. Why not take our interest, dividends, and capital gains and move those earnings to some other part of our Financial Treatment Plan and make another use of that dollar. Each time we make another use of a dollar we gain increased benefits and additional rates of return. We will actually verify this money strategy in our "Money Myths Debunked" chapter (chapter 4) when we discuss an alternative to compounding interest.

Keeping money in motion is all about getting multiple uses out of every dollar and not letting any dollar die by sitting too long in one spot in the Financial Treatment Plan. Allowing your money to sit in one place too long is like having a blood clot in the body that prevents the blood from flowing through your organs! Blood clots cause heart attacks and strokes. If you have stale or stagnant money in your personal finances, you are placing your present and future financial situation on life support! This is one of the many reasons why the average dentist retires with a 50 percent pay cut in retirement.

Think of it as a chess game. Every chess piece has different strengths and powers, just as every financial product has advantages and disadvantages. The objective of chess is to get to checkmate in the shortest number of moves possible in order to win the match. No single move or chess piece will win the game. Rather, games are won through a series of moves that strategically position many chess pieces in order to secure a victory. As an example, the queen is the most powerful chess piece on the board. However, if that is all you have on the board, you will not win the game. The game of finance is much like chess in that you will need multiple financial products that are strategically placed and in constant motion. It is this type of game play that will help you achieve your full wealth potential and avoid a pay cut in retirement.

Instead of being taught the money chess game, dentists have been taught to put their money in one place and let it sit, as, for example, in a retirement plan. In doing so, they are handcuffing their money, because once it goes into that retirement plan, it is locked up until the dentists are fifty-nine and a half years of age. Once that dollar goes in, they're never going to get another use out of it throughout their accumulation period. This is very inefficient. To be clear, though, we are not saying that retirement plans are bad. Instead, we are saying that you need to understand the ramifications of putting money into that type of account as a first move of your money.

Also, dentists are taught to focus on achieving high returns in their investments, which, oftentimes, causes them to chase a rate of return to their detriment. Contrary to the popular opinion of investment advisors, the rate of return is not nearly as important as you think. Why? Because the existence of wealth-eroding factors in a Financial Treatment Plan will have a far bigger impact than a rate of return will ever have on your wealth. These wealth-eroding factors attack your money twenty-four hours a day, seven days a week, each and every year of your life. The ramifications of taxes and inflation are two of the better-known wealth-eroding factors that people face daily. Most people already understand how these factors negatively affect their wealth, but there are a number of other factors that also impact wealth.

In fact, upward of 12 percent of your money is being eroded away on a yearly basis due to taxes, inflation, planned obsolescence, technological change, and unexpected life events. This means you have to save at least 12 percent each year just to overcome these wealth-eroding factors alone. In order to outpace these basic effects of wealth erosion, you must establish the discipline of saving a minimum of 15 percent of your income each year. If you do not save at this rate, then you are going backward.

The object of keeping your money in motion is to pick up individual rates of return and increased benefits each time you turn, or move, the money. With each move you may get 5 percent here, 5 percent there and 5 percent over there. Add those up and you're getting a 15 percent rate of return with less risk and more benefit. Again, this velocity of money principle will be highlighted in the compound interest example discussed in chapter 4, "Money Myths Debunked." Investors in this day and age find a 5 percent rate of return decent, but 5 percent taken multiple times with increased benefits is a home-run investment.

We hear the question all the time: What rate of return are your investments getting? If this is your primary concern, I can share with you that you're asking the wrong question. Your question should be, How am I going to overcome the wealth eroders of life and do so with less risk? If you *only* focused on overcoming wealth-eroding factors, you would achieve success beyond your wildest dreams.

Because dentists are smart, some dentists believe they can manage their own money. After all, there's a lot of financial information out in the media today to help do-it-yourselfers make financial decisions. For example, at Fidelity.com, you can read that if you have eight times your salary saved by age sixty, you are on the right track. So, let's put some numbers to this advice and assume you are making $500,000 a year, prior to retirement. According to this advice you would then only need $4,000,000 of saved assets when you retire. Again, using the traditional world's advice for retirement income planning, you would then take a 3 percent safe withdrawal from these assets for an annual retirement income of $120,000. If you are a do-it-yourselfer and follow this advice, you will set yourself up to take about a 75 percent pay cut in retirement! This is one of the reasons why we are adamant that do-it-yourselfers will struggle to reach their full wealth potential.

You can go online and find different financial calculators for retirement. With each one, you can input how much money will be saved on an annual basis, your expected rate of return, and the number of years you have before you retire. Click the magic button and you are told how much money you will have when you retire. If this final retirement sum is not enough, you have one of two choices: either save more money or chase a higher rate of return. If you can't save more money, you then simply plug in a higher rate of return until you get the result you want, as though you are guaranteed to realize the higher rate of return. Even if this is guaranteed, you have now assumed much more risk and volatility in your planning, but you feel better because you are now on track for retirement.

This is not retirement planning! It's just playing math games with numbers until you get a result you like. It is the proverbial massaging of the numbers for financial comfort. Online calculators are a detriment to your long-term financial health. They often provide a false sense of security, indicating that your financial plan is on track for success. Unfortunately, they are an essential planning tool for the do-it-yourselfer.

If you look at truly successful people, whether they are in business, sports, or entertainment, almost every one of them has a coach. For example, a golfer may have several coaches: a swing coach, a physical trainer, and a putting instructor. It's possible there might even be a sports psychologist on board to help the golfer deal with the mental aspects of the game.

Why is it, then, that dentists fight the idea of having a financial coach to help them navigate the confusing world of personal finance?

Too often, the reason dentists are disappointed with their financial portfolios is because their advisors have only focused these portfolios on accumulating assets that are driven by a rate of return. Focusing on the accumulation of assets leads to frustration as markets fluctuate and returns are not what were expected. As a result, many dentists will make the decision to just do it themselves. Financial success, however, is not a rate of return equation. Rate of return is only *part* of the puzzle.

Financial success is having the maximum benefits from a maximum money supply at all times in your life. This is the foundation for what creates enjoyment in dentists' lives, ultimately a retirement where they do not take pay cuts and have guarantees built in to their retirement incomes. The guarantees are what provide immense peace of mind to dentists in retirement, because no matter what happens, they know with certainty that they will never run out of money.

As we have discussed, the rainmakers are fighting for your money, so you need to know how to counterpunch and not sit back and let your wealth be eroded away. The great philosopher Mike Tyson once said, "Everyone has a plan until they get punched in the mouth!" By understanding that the rules the rainmakers follow are different from the rules they promote for you and me as consumers, you will have significantly more wealth than the average dentist and avoid being knocked out financially. It is the old saying: if you can't beat them, join them.

One of our many objectives is to help you discover how to live by the same rules as the rainmakers. It is our hope that we will expose you to eye-opening information when it comes to your personal finances and get you excited about a macroeconomic model for your money. Let's start by looking at the big money picture.

Chapter 2

THE BIG MONEY PICTURE

• • •

May you find INSPIRATION in the big picture,
but may you find LOVE in the details.

—ADRIENNE MALOOF

t has been reported that six in ten baby boomers feared running out of money before they died more than death itself.[6] Even though dentists make a lot of money during their working years, they are no different in regard to their anxieties. They, too, fear running out of money. Developing strategies to position dentists to hold multiple income streams in retirement creates a bulletproof plan, so that no matter what happens, they *can't* run out of money. This takes that fear off the table!

According to the IRS, multimillionaires will have, on average, seven different sources of income in retirement. Unfortunately, the majority of dentists who retire will only have three to four income streams. If you reduce the stress brought on by fear, your health will

---

6   Catey Hill, "Older people fear this more than death," MarketWatch, July 21, 2016, https://www.marketwatch.com/story/older-people-fear-this-more-than-death-2016-07-18.

most likely improve. You're better psychologically and physically. You may even live longer. Peace of mind is priceless.

To help our clients gain that peace of mind, we begin by looking at what we call the big picture. In the big money picture, there are three wealth-building phases: accumulation, distribution, and preservation, all of which are supported by a *wrapper*. The traditional financial world looks at the three phases of wealth building as if they occur in a linear pattern: one after the other. The reality is that every financial decision a person makes, whether that person is young or old, can and does have an impact on at least two if not all three phases of wealth building *simultaneously*. This is critically important to understand. Financial decisions are dynamic. A decision regarding accumulation doesn't just affect the accumulation of your wealth; it also affects the distribution and preservation of your money at the same time. That is one of the big disconnects between what we do as macroadvisors, and what traditional microfinancial advisors do. We make sure we account for each of these phases in every decision that our dental clients make.

The three wealth phases—accumulation, distribution, and preservation—have historically been presented to us as individual phases we encounter, based on age. The accumulation phase, which is all about accruing or growing wealth, is normally thought to be the period of time during our working career leading to retirement. Frequently, in the traditional world of finance, we are led to believe that the accumulation phase stops at retirement. Why can't the accumulation phase continue throughout our entire lifetime? Accomplishing lifelong accumulation would be the ideal and something that every dentist would want.

In the traditional world of finance, the wealth distribution phase is thought to cover the period of twenty to thirty years called retirement. We believe the time horizon of this wealth phase is actually much longer, starting early in dentists' careers and continuing until their death. This is due to our definition of wealth distribution, which defines this phase as the spending and enjoyment of personal assets both today and in the future without the fear of ever running out of money.

In other words, how do you position yourself to have maximum retirement income with guarantees in the future and still enjoy life to the fullest today? This could mean owning a second home at the lake or on the beach now rather than later. Wouldn't you want to do this and more while working and know with certainty that your retirement is secure? Having a retirement plan with no distribution strategy to fully enjoy your earnings is not retirement planning. Discussions about your wealth distribution strategies and desires should start during your working years and continue throughout your lifetime. As a matter of fact, an important question that you should ask and answer prior to making any investment is, How am I going to get this money out in the future to enjoy?

The preservation phase, in the traditional world, represents the time at the end of your life. This is a time when assets are hopefully passed on intact to loved ones or charity. Unfortunately, due to ineffective planning throughout a dentist's life, more of a dentist's wealth is passed on to the government in the form of unnecessary taxes, and to corporations (e.g., long-term-care facilities), financial institutions, and lastly, other wealthy people (e.g., fire/estate, sales). Again, just like the previous two wealth phases, accumulation and distribution, the preservation phase should be addressed and considered with each financial decision during a dentist's lifetime.

Traditional financial planners look at each of these three phases as singular phases of life. Yet, every decision has lasting effects that impact all three phases, regardless of age. This is why it is so important to know the impact on each wealth phase—accumulation, distribution, and preservation—when making financial decisions. Again, this is another reason why a macroeconomic model, such as the Financial Treatment Plan, is so important to financial well-being.

For example, you can make a solid accumulation decision, such as funding a retirement plan, and pick up some tax advantages by doing so. You will get a pretax deduction on the contribution and your growth on the investment is tax deferred, both good things. But too often there is no thought given to how you are going to get that money out of the retirement plan. If you wait until retirement to make that distribution decision, by default you have put shackles on how much you will be able to actually enjoy your wealth in your later years. Remember the 50 percent pay-cut discussion? Since you did not make an exit strategy ahead of time, you will be left with significantly less income in retirement—in the neighborhood of a 50 percent loss of income for the average dentist!

Understanding how the different phases interact with each other is essential, but it also important to have wealth objectives that are coordinated with each of the phases. We call this a financial mission statement. Most dentists will have a mission statement for their practice but never consider having one for their personal finances. A mission statement is nothing more than a statement of purpose. When a dentist has a financial mission statement for building wealth, financial decisions can be made with confidence if the money decisions align with the mission's stated purpose. The following four objectives make up the financial mission statement. We use these as a framework to overcome the emotions and opinions that come with every financial decision. These objectives/mission statement are the first step in peace of mind planning.

FIRST OBJECTIVE: BUILD WEALTH EFFICIENTLY WITH LESS RISK

Our first objective is to help dentists maximize the building of their wealth in the most efficient manner possible without increasing risk. Again, that is counterintuitive to the traditional world of finance because we have all been led to believe that if we want more wealth, we have to take more risk and chase a higher rate of return. If a plan is efficient, an overall high rate of return will be achieved in the macroeconomic model with less risk. Understanding the strategy behind financial products and how to properly use them in combination with one another as part of your Financial Treatment Plan drives efficiency. Embracing this philosophy will create additional wealth for you by making use of the same dollars in your present financial plan but not taking additional risk.

In order to increase efficiency, you need to keep your money in motion, as the rainmakers do. By doing so, you can use the same inputs that you are already utilizing and not change your present lifestyle. Your standard of living stays the same. We decrease the waste and offset some of the eroding factors, such as taxes and inflation. By reengineering the flow of these dollars, you will have an increased money supply and gain additional benefits. This is the real differentiator that will take you to that next level of wealth creation. Always remember that the longer your money stagnates (by sitting in one place), the more you are reducing the overall efficiency of your plan. You have to keep your money moving!

A perfect financial plan is a series of one-year perfect plans that need to be fine-tuned annually. Think of it as being like car maintenance. If you take care of your car, it will last longer. On the other hand, if you don't take care of your car—by skipping a tune-up or maybe changing your oil less frequently than recommended—then your car is going to deteriorate much faster than it would on a regular maintenance schedule.

The efficient approach is to have the car serviced periodically: oil change, spark plugs, tire rotation, fluid check, and so on. After servicing the car, you get the same car back, but it operates more efficiently. Simple maintenance of a car allows it to perform better and last longer. We want to do the same with your money from an efficiency standpoint so that the same dollars give you greater financial output now and in the long run.

The concept of buying a car and driving it for five years with no regular maintenance is similar to the traditional world's approach to your financial life. Within the dental world, the conventional wisdom is to maximize your qualified retirement plan contributions through a 401(k)/profit-sharing plan. Then, if you are contributing the maximum and you still have excess funds to save, your advisor may tell you to add a cash balance plan. Depending on how the cash balance plan is structured you may be able to contribute upward of another couple hundred thousand dollars or more. Now your money just sits there in a retirement investment account with occasional asset allocation changes and waits for you to retire. In other words, it stagnates! You think you're doing the right thing, but the truth is that a retirement plan by itself will result in very few retirement income options. It is the old proverbial adage of putting all your eggs in one basket. Very inefficient!

Another traditional inefficient approach is dollar cost averaging (DCA) into after-tax plans. DCA is an investment technique that involves buying a fixed dollar amount of a particular investment on a regular schedule, regardless of the share price. This is all about accumulating assets with no regard to what the exit or distribution strategy will be. Nor are the many eroding factors involved considered.

Nobody is talking to you about the negative effects that go along with these traditional decisions. The reality is that every financial decision you make will have negative as well as positive effects. There is no one perfect product. If there were, we'd all buy it and we would all be wealthy. The key is being as efficient as possible in accentuating the positive effects and mitigating the negative ones.

In order to be successful in your financial life, you must have balance. If you place too much weight on any one area of your financial life—whether it is in a retirement plan, investments, real estate, or life insurance—at the expense of the other areas, you are susceptible to future problems. You need to have balance. Having balance always results in less risk in your financial life.

Traditionally, risk is associated with a higher rate of return, which is just *one* of many factors that will determine your eventual wealth. Those who focus *only* on a rate of return to drive the success of their financial plan will be disappointed at some point due to their heavy reliance on market results. As we all know, the stock market cannot be controlled. The market will go up and it will go down; we never know how to time it effectively. Unknowns, such as flying a plane into the World Trade Center or an interest rate adjustment by the Federal Reserve will impact the stock market. We cannot change that.

Another factor that impacts your wealth-building capability is your annual savings rate. If you are not disciplined and saving at least 15 percent each year, it doesn't matter if you get a 20 percent rate of return on your money. A small savings amount, despite a high rate of return, still does not end up being that much. The most important factor in wealth building is the ability to save as much money as you can. If you can't save, it will be almost impossible to achieve financial success regardless of the rate of return earned. You will also work much longer than you want to.

Many times, when we work with dentists, they talk about their investment successes but rarely mention their investment losses. Yet, 46 percent of orthodontists felt that money lost due to investments was a barrier to being financially prepared for retirement.[7] The reality is that you will experience both successes and failures in your financial life. As such, for financial success to occur you must maximize the wins and minimizing the losses. If you earn 10 percent on one investment and take a loss in another investment, this is not a 10 percent win. Your net gain or loss is a combination of the two investment results. Therefore, the rate of return on any one investment does not determine your financial state. As much as your present advisors may tell you that investment rate of return is important, it is just another part of your financial equation.

When people chase the rate of return, they end up shooting themselves in the foot because they are focused solely on what the market is doing or not doing. For example, as we write this book, we have had an incredible bull run in the markets, but at some point in the future, there will be a market correction. When that occurs, panic for some will set in, especially for those who have small cash positions for liquidity. Dentists in this situation are caught in the position of having to get out of the market because they don't have the cash reserves to stomach a big loss. As the well-respected investor Larry Swedroe (director of research, BAM Alliance) said, "I've yet to meet a stomach that makes good decisions."

Dentists who are caught in this situation and sell in a low market often end up with their money on the sidelines in a money market account. They often have no idea of when to reinvest in the market. This unknown can cost them a ton of money. No one has a crystal

---

7   Jeremiah Sturgill and Jae Park, "Changes in Orthodontists' Retirement Planning and Practice Operations Due to the Recent Recession."

ball forecasting the right moment to get back into the investing game. What's going to be your cue? When the market goes down? If yes, how far does the market need to go down before you get back in? And how much are you going to reinvest?

When you do make the decision to get back in the market, you may buy back in at a higher position than you initially sold. If that is the case, you missed out on some gains by delaying your reentry into the market. This is why chasing a rate of return without having a real investment strategy for your plan is not likely to be a successful journey. It is truly an exercise in futility, yet, everyone does it, and so it must be correct, right? Wrong!

A well-respected investment study on market returns was conducted by Dalbar. The table on the next page shows that the S&P 500 has delivered a market rate of return of 5.62 percent over the past twenty years. The average investor over that same time period only received a return of 3.88 percent. This represents a 31 percent difference between what the S&P 500 actually delivered in the market versus what the average investor received. For many, this will translate into hundreds of thousands—if not millions—of dollars of lost wealth. In this case, the 1.74 percent difference in rate of return that was lost is due primarily to the emotions experienced by investors who didn't have a strategic way of looking at their investments.

WHY DO ACTIVE INVESTORS FAIL?

	ANNUALIZED RETURN
S&P 500 Index	5.62%
Average Equity Fund Investor	3.88%
Bloomberg Barclays Aggregate Bond Index	5.29%
Average Fixed Income Fund Investor	0.48%
Average Equity Fund Investor Holding Period	3.5 Years

Source: "DALBAR 2018 QAIB—Quantitative Analysis of Investor Behavior, covering the period of January 1, 1997 through December 31, 2016," DALBAR, https://svwealth.com/wp-content/uploads/2018/04/dalbar_study.pdf.[8]

Table 2.1

Keep in mind that any market rate of return presented to you is either based on a projection of anticipated future results or past performance. Nobody knows what the future holds, and by no means is this projection a guarantee of what you will actually receive.

---

8   Dalbar is the financial community's leading independent expert in evaluating, auditing, and rating business practices, customer performance, product quality, and service. Launched in 1976, Dalbar has earned recognition for consistent and unbiased evaluations of investment companies, registered investment advisers, insurance companies, broker/dealers, retirement plan providers and financial professionals. (Dalbar.com)

Also, when evaluating the merits of a financial decision, you must consider the other variables or benefits that result from that decision, such as whether there are tax ramifications. Are you picking up a disability benefit? Is there a premature death benefit or better yet a living benefit? Will you receive a tax deduction, a tax deferral, or tax-free access on your funds? Are the funds liquid or are they locked up? Can you get to them prior to fifty-nine and a half? In other words, if you want to make good financial decisions, you must account for all of the advantages and disadvantages surrounding that decision and not just consider the potential rate of return.

An efficient Financial Treatment Plan is judged by the sum of all of its parts. It is not just a rate of return or any one variable or benefit resulting from a financial decision that makes a plan great. Instead, it is all of these things that allow us to create wealth efficiently and with less risk.

SECOND OBJECTIVE: SPEND *AND* ENJOY YOUR WEALTH WITHOUT THE FEAR OF RUNNING OUT OF MONEY

Our second objective deals with the distribution phase of wealth enhancement. A properly designed distribution phase allows dentists to have their cake and eat it too. This powerful objective is aimed at allowing our clients to be able to fully spend and enjoy their wealth today, as well as in the future, *without* the fear of running out of funds.

In the traditional world of financial planning, the distribution phase of life is concentrated on retirement. Traditional planners of all types typically tell you that you get to enjoy your money after you retire. Your career as a dentist has spanned thirty to forty years, during which time you have hopefully acquired some wealth. Did you work and set money aside to enjoy in retirement only? We hope not, for it's possible that an accident or illness may prevent you from ever seeing retirement. Mart's father passed away at the age of sixty-five after working for more than thirty years for IBM. Did he get to enjoy his retirement? The answer is an emphatic no! We want our clients to have the freedom as well as the permission to spend and enjoy their wealth both today and in the future.

For instance, if you want to own a second home, be it on the lake, the beach, or in the mountains, why wait until you retire? Why not make that purchase when your kids are young and still want to spend time with you? That's the time to create family memories. Purchasing a second home when our children were young is one of the best things we have done for our families. What do you think the rate of return has been on those investments? The rate of return from enjoyment has been infinite!

The traditional financial world scares you by saying that if you are not putting money away through investments, you will not have enough money in the future for your retirement. That's what we call a scarcity mentality. Remember traditional planners live in a world of assets under management. Their advice preys on fear and guilt. They also benefit from a client mind-set of maintaining the status quo or minimal change. In the end, advisors manage a lot of money in retirement accounts, while dentists receive little enjoyment during their working years from that same money.

Our mind-set works in total opposition to the strategies of traditional planners. We want to help you develop a financial life that allows you to fully enjoy your money when you are young and healthy, and at the same time gets you to the retirement stage with full income replacement. Better yet, we want your retirement income to have guarantees built in that ensure your money will never run out.

Saving, investing, and spending are not mutually exclusive things. Almost every dentist we meet is making maximum contributions to a qualified plan. Today (2019), dentists under the age of fifty can contribute a maximum of $56,000 a year to their 401(k), safe-harbor, and profit-sharing plan. If the dentists are fifty or older, they can contribute a maximum of $62,000 to these plans. That's a lot of money. Again, once it goes into the retirement plan, it is in prison. Dentists can't access it prior to age fifty-nine and a half without paying hefty penalties or dealing with a convoluted process. The retirement plan is not liquid, and is solely dependent upon what the market does or does not do. Even worse, dentists are getting only one use out of that money over many years, and that is never good.

Instead of throwing all of your money into a retirement plan, why not max out the employee and safe harbor contributions of $19,000 and $11,200, respectively. The retirement plan is now funded with $30,200 for the year. That leaves $25,800 that would have gone into profit sharing if you had elected to fund the plan. In addition, if you suspend your profit-sharing-plan contribution, you may save another $6,000 to $8,000 that would have gone to other employees. You now have up to $33,800 that you can take as a distribution. Of course, taxes must be paid on this amount, but this sum could go a long way in supporting a mortgage on a second home.

For the same dollars, you now have a retirement plan *and* a second home to enjoy. If the second home is located in a vacation destination area, perhaps it could be rented out when you are not using it, which creates another income stream. It really is like having your cake and eating it too. You have your retirement plan for later, and a second home to enjoy today. You also may have created an income-producing asset, and guess what? Real estate in areas where second homes are located tend to appreciate over time. Down the road, if you elect to sell the second home, the appreciation is treated as a capital gain, which is taxed at 15–20 percent today. This is opposed to all gains in a retirement plan that are taxed at the highest ordinary income tax bracket that you fall into at the time of withdrawal. Today that rate could be as high as 37 percent. This is a great example of a win-win strategy where the two objectives of investing in a retirement plan and enjoying your earnings today were addressed with the same money.

Everyone loves this objective because dentists can have their cake and eat it too. We believe that people don't make money to hoard it, but to enjoy it! With that in mind, there needs to be built-in strategies to overcome the greatest fear people face in retirement: running out of money. Therefore, guarantees are built in to the Financial Treatment Plan for ultimate peace of mind in retirement. Enjoy your cake!

THIRD OBJECTIVE: ENJOY YOUR WEALTH AND PASS ON THE REST

Our third objective deals with the preservation or conservation of your wealth. If we have followed the macrofinancial blueprint well and created maximum wealth in the Financial Treatment Plan over a lifetime, then there is going to be money left over for loved ones or charities in the future. At the end of your life, your money can only go to one of six places: the government, financial institutions, corporations, other wealthy people, your family, or charities.

Of those six, where do most dentists want to see their wealth go? The answer is, obviously, to family, charities, or both. The unfortunate thing is that due to improper planning, more wealth gets transferred to those first four groups than it does to family or charities. The takeaway is this: if you want your wealth to go to your family and/or charities, then you need to plan for that to happen.

Most dentists have a charitable intent. They would like to see some of their wealth go to charity, but for most, this does not happen, because they are afraid they won't have enough money to live on in retirement. They're not sure how long they're going to live, and many are not sure how to make a sizable charitable gift other than, maybe, a gift at death.

Often, dentists (including most advisors) don't understand the powerful charitable giving strategies that are available to them. The number-one form of charitable giving is writing a check and taking the deduction on your tax return that year. In doing so, you only get one benefit from that transaction, which is the tax deduction on the donation. Why not utilize a simple strategy that we call turbotithe. This straightforward strategy will be discussed in greater detail in chapter 8. It's like hitting a triple instead of a single in baseball.

The *most* powerful charitable strategy, however, is a planning strategy that encompasses a number of financial moves. First, it positions dentists to give to charity while not disinheriting loved ones or family members. Most importantly, dentists will receive increased retirement income over and above what they would have received if they had not given to charity. It is a triple win for the charity, the dentists' heirs, and the dentists, as donors. It is a unique strategy that gets everyone excited. More on this later in the book!

The triple win may seem counterintuitive to ordinary thinking, but it is possible. Everybody thinks that giving money away to a charity means having less in total assets. Thus, their income is reduced because the assets that were given to the charity are no longer producing income. If you simply write a check as a one-time donation, this is true. But if you have a strategic charitable plan, the act of giving can create income while you're alive and you will not disinherit the family.

We also believe that there is an enjoyment to giving to charity while you're alive rather than just designating assets to a charity after you die. When you arrange for your donations to be made after your death, you never get to see the benefits of your generosity. The best time to give to charity is when you are young because you will be able to see the benefits of your gift, which also include the fact that when you are more giving, you tend to be happier.

If the majority of dentists choose family and friends as their legacy choices, why does most of their money end up going to the first four groups?

If the estate is large enough, there could be estate taxes paid to the government unnecessarily. There can also be taxes paid upon death that could have been avoided with proper planning. Therefore, the government wins and you lose. Incurring significant long-term care expenses certainly makes corporations rich and depletes estates, which reduces the amount that can be passed on to family or charities. Without proper planning, the elderly can pass an extraordinary amount of wealth to a long-term-care facility at the end of their life. In a worst-case scenario, the house you thought you were going to leave to your kids ends up going to the state as reimbursement for Medicaid nursing home payments. Even if the house remains in the possession of your family, often the estate has, basically, been spent down to nothing because there was no long-term-care strategy in place. Therefore, the corporations win and you lose!

With inefficient products in place, financial institutions will continue to erode your wealth with high fees or low rates of return paid on your investments. Over an extended period of time this can reduce the amount of your estate and what you ultimately pass on to loved ones or charities when you die. Once again, financial institutions win and you lose!

Finally, other wealthy people can benefit from the fire sale of the possessions in your estate.

These are just some of the examples of what can happen when you have not properly planned in the preservation phase: Wealth is often lost, and families and charities are the biggest losers. The winners should be your family and your chosen charities, not the other groups!

FOURTH WEALTH OBJECTIVE: THE WRAPPER

Dentists love our first three wealth objectives aimed at creating maximum wealth without increased risk, being able to spend and enjoy their maximum wealth without the fear of running out of money in retirement, and then ensuring that their legacies go to family and charities. We've never had any dentists tell us that they don't want these objectives.

Our fourth objective, which we refer to as the wrapper, ties everything together. It is simply this: failure is not an option. In other words, you have to have contingency plans in place to offset all the various life events that can and do happen throughout our lifetime. Most financial plans are based on a best-case scenario, and if you draw that picture on a spreadsheet, it always looks good. They assume, for example, that dentists will always receive a consistent and high rate of return on their investments year in and year out; tax rates will never change; and dentists and their families will never encounter a health or family crisis that requires a monetary outlay to address the crisis. What about a disability, premature death, or some other career disruption that drains resources? You will be sadly disappointed at some point if your financial plan's success is contingent on a best-case scenario only.

The problem is that life happens. We all experience both good and bad life events. With that in mind we should build financial plans that will be successful under *all* circumstances. Failure cannot be an option! Financial Treatment Plans need to address all ways that failure can creep into the plan. When a Financial Treatment Plan is properly structured for success, there is no cost differential between having a financial plan that is built on the best-case scenario versus a plan that's built on the worst-case scenario. So if costs were the same, why wouldn't we want to have success ensured under the worst-case scenario since the best-case scenario never happens?

When a Financial Treatment Plan is built in this fashion and a worst-case scenario occurs, your plan is still going to be successful. Also, anything better than the worst-case scenario will be icing on the cake. Perhaps you will live a charmed life and never experience a negative life event. Keep in mind, however, that even one unforeseen event that is not planned for could bring down your financial house if your financial plan is only based on best-case scenarios.

• • • • • • • • • • • • • • • • • • •

Mart

I had open-heart surgery at age forty-five due to an undiagnosed congenital heart valve defect. That's not a normal thing, right? You don't expect that. Nobody in their right mind would assume they would have open-heart surgery at age forty-five. When I was wheeled into the operating room, I was very aware that I might not make it out alive.

Thankfully, my Financial Treatment Plan was positioned in such a way that if anything had happened to me, I knew with 100 percent certainty that my wife and kids would be totally fine financially for the rest of their lives. Knowing this, I went into surgery with total peace of mind and less worry, which I believe helped lower my stress and improve my overall recovery process. Those are the plans we like to build for our clients.

• • • • • • • • • • • • • • • • • • •

• • • • • • • • • • • • • • • • • • •

Tim

Early in my career, during the decade of the 1990s, the stock market had one of its best runs ever. The annualized return in the S&P 500 for that decade was almost 18 percent. Then we had the dot-com bust followed by the September 11 terrorist attack, which dramatically impacted the markets from 2000 to 2002. For many invested in the market, this was a very unsettling time.

In late 2002, I was introduced to a dentist who had retired at the end of 1999 with over $4 million in his retirement plan. When this dentist initially retired, he thought he had more than enough money to live on. Then the market crashed. At the time I was introduced to the dentist, his original $4 million retirement account was now less than $2 million. He was sixty-two years old and healthy, with a long life in front of him. His money was supposed to provide him and his wife with an income stream for the rest of their lives. Now with the down market and only three years into retirement, he felt he had to go back to work, downsize his home, and sell his second home. He was not positioned properly. A market crash not only impacted his retirement plan but also added stress to his life at a time when he didn't need it.

Unfortunately, there are far too many stories just like this, involving dentists who have retired without locking in guaranteed income streams. Without guarantees in retirement, it only takes one little thing to upset the apple cart, and then the domino effect takes over. It does not have to be this way.

• • • • • • • • • • • • • • • • • • •

Since we have all experienced some setbacks in our financial lives, we need to be proactive and not reactive in casting those setbacks as mere blips on the radar and not devastations. When all contingencies are accounted for in a Financial Treatment Plan, dentists do not have to be reactive when a worst-case scenario occurs, as it is already addressed in their plan. This provides tremendous peace of mind to dentists, as they know they will be okay no matter what happens.

While traditional planners may only talk about the best-case scenario because it is an easier sell, the other factor at work is simply human nature. People are, generally, positive, and we tend to believe that bad things only happen to other people. Unfortunately, when bad things do happen to us, it's too late to make personal preparations. No one has a crystal ball and no matter what we think, life can change at the blink of an eye. We can get in our car today and unintentionally cause an accident by going through a red light that we did not see at an intersection. If that accident causes a disability or death, do you think that will change your financial life? The answer is yes, if you are not properly protected.

As a dentist, whether you have accumulated some wealth at this point in your life or not, you are actually more vulnerable to a lawsuit than the average Joe. Unfortunately, you're a target with a bull's-eye on your back due to having the word *doctor* in front of your name. If a situation such as a car accident were to occur and an attorney were to become involved, you can be certain that you would find yourself in court.

This is where the wrapper or Financial Treatment Plan comes into play. In order for a Financial Treatment Plan to be effective, it must be able to stress-test any conceivable scenario or financial decision. A Financial Treatment Plan allows dentists to measure the impact of a lawsuit, a disability, a premature death, unexpected emergency, and funding for college, to name a few situations. In addition, tax law changes, market fluctuations, and interest rate movements are also measured. The Financial Treatment Plan has the power to measure any one of these variables either by itself or in different combinations.

The Financial Treatment Plan gives us a process whereby we can analyze any decision *before* we actually take action. This is how we can build plans that work under all circumstances. We stress-test situations before implementing them to determine if this is the way we want to go or not. Financial alternatives are tested in the Financial Treatment Plan much as a pilot uses a flight simulator to test different flight situations. It is a proactive process, not reactive. We call it evidence-based financial planning or planning with confidence.

The ability to test and measure different financial scenarios before committing to a financial decision is a difference maker. The Financial Treatment Plan allows dentists to fully measure all of the positive and negative aspects associated with a planning decision and verify expected output on the back end. Another great thing about the Financial Treatment Plan is that dentists can totally customize it to what they want.

A yearly review and update of the dentist's Financial Treatment Plan will help ensure its long-term success. As we discussed earlier, life will change often, and it is important that the Financial Treatment Plan is flexible enough to adapt to any new life changes or events. Changes to the Financial Treatment Plan are simpler to make when the plan is updated annually. On the other hand, drastic decisions may have to be made when yearly reviews are ignored.

Typically, when we meet with dentists, we ask them if there is anything about these wealth objectives that they disagree with. If not, then the next step is to take action and learn more about how the Financial Treatment Plan can be applied in their situation. These objectives become our financial mission statement for everyone we work with. As such, all potential financial decisions are measured against this statement and if they meet its objectives, the dentist will take action of them. If not, they are discarded.

What makes our Financial Treatment Plan unique and different from a traditional financial plan is that the success of our planning process is not dependent upon a magic financial product or investment, or even a single strategy. Also, traditional financial plans fall short by looking at planning considerations such as retirement planning, college planning, debt repayment, and estate planning, to name a few, as individual events. In reality, each of these events affects each other simultaneously. The traditional world has no mechanism like our Financial Treatment Plan to simultaneously measure the impacts of these huge decisions.

In short, financial success is derived from having a Financial Treatment Plan and a rulebook that is based on economic principles in order to measure and analyze financial decisions. It is also imperative that you have a macroadvisor on your team to assist you in sorting through the misinformation, sales hype, and opinion that is rampant in the financial world today. All three need to be present in order to succeed.

We certainly hope these four wealth objectives resonate with you. These are our core values. They enable us to create plans that can work under all circumstances and prevent a pay cut in retirement, which means more life enjoyment.

Chapter 3

EVEN THE LONE RANGER HAD TONTO

• • •

Coaching is taking a player where they can't take themself.

—JOSE MOURINHO

The Lone Ranger was a fictional Western character who fought outlaws with his friend Tonto in the very popular TV series of the same name that ran on ABC from 1949 to 1957. Tonto called the Lone Ranger Kemo Sabe, which means "faithful friend" or "trusty scout." They were a team who fought the bad guys and they needed each other to succeed. Due to all the faulty premises in the world of personal finance, dentists need a faithful and trusted advisor whom they can work with on their journeys toward ultimate financial success. Everyone should have a financial Kemo Sabe!

Dentists graduate from dental school with little to no information or training on how to start a business or manage their money. On top of that, most dental graduates today will likely carry student loan debt in the hundreds of thousands of dollars. Although daunting, you still feel this is a situation you can handle. After all, the fact that you were accepted into dental school proves that you are smart.

The question is, Does this intelligence automatically translate into financial intelligence? From our experience, the answer is no. This is normal, however, because your dental education did not include training in economics or personal finance.

Ask successful athletes what it takes to make it to the next level and they will say a great coach or coaches. Professional athletes use coaches to develop their skills and make them champions. Michael Jordan is the greatest basketball player ever. Tom Brady is the only football player to win six Super Bowls. Serena Williams is the foremost woman tennis player in history. Not one of these athletes achieved their level of success alone. Olympic athletes have multiple coaches. As do professionals in other fields: singers, actors, musicians, CEOs, and entrepreneurs. Even the best dentists have mentors or take continuing education courses to enhance their skills.

So the question should not be, "why do you need help managing your money?" but rather, "why do you think you *don't* need help managing your money?" You may understand basic financial principles, but do you get the nuances? Once your practice is up and running, will you have time to spend monitoring a successful financial plan? You can keep up with your continuing education credits, but do you also have the hours to put into studying new tax laws, reading about the latest financial products, and monitoring the stock market? Are you sure your emotions about money aren't clouding your decisions? Also, are you positive a different perspective won't add to your financial success?

If you are a dentist, you are in the office from eight in the morning until six at night and you are almost always with patients. So when would you have the time to manage your finances? Weekends? Do you really want to spend your weekends pouring over numbers? No you don't, which is why *you* want a coach.

Yet, almost half (46.2 percent) of orthodontists make their own financial decisions and there are websites and blogs that say you should do it yourself. As dentists, we are commonly asked by our patients about techniques and products that they read about online. A lot of that information has no substance or is unfounded, yet people believe it is true because it is on the web. The same goes with personal financial advice. There is a popular blog and website for health professionals that has a course titled "Fire Your Financial Advisor: A Step-By-Step Process to Creating and Implementing Your Own Financial Plan." After finishing our book, you will clearly see that most of the information online and in the media pertaining to financial planning will turn the white coat of the doctor red!

As macroeconomic advisors, our relationship with dental clients is similar to that of a National Football League (NFL) owner with his head coach. The owner brings in a head coach to partner in developing a great team. The head coach holds the ultimate responsibility for putting a winning team on the field. To accomplish this objective, the head coach will work with an offensive coordinator, a defensive coordinator, and a special teams coach. The head coach will also work with other coaches who each specialize in a player position, such as quarterback, lineman, running back, receiver, and others. Together, the efforts of these coaches will build a winning game plan under the direction and leadership of the head coach. It is the head coach's responsibility to make sure that all aspects of the game plan are coordinated so that success can be achieved.

Bringing in those assistant coaches is similar to the macroadvisor working with an accountant, attorney, a bank's lending officer, or investment advisor to build the dentist's financial team. Each one of these microadvisors will be skilled in one or two areas of an individual's personal financial plan, as are the quarterback and defensive line coaches for an NFL team. The microadvisors will bring their ideas to the table, but it is the macroadvisor's job to blend these ideas together to create a game plan for the dentist's financial success. This is similar to the head coach utilizing the skills of his assistant coaches to create a winning team.

A problem we see in the dental world is that financial opinions often get in the way of economic facts, especially if the approach is traditional. Accountants base their opinions about what's financially best for you on their training. The same goes for investment advisors. They are going to focus on investments but don't necessarily see how those investments affect other aspects of your financial life. The ultimate result is skewed in the direction of your advisors' expertise and internal bias. Unfortunately, most dentists will hire an advisor who has the best sales pitch or strongest opinion. Parents, family, and friends of the dentist can also have a lot of influence on their decisions. As tough as it may be, you work very hard for your money. You and your family have to live with the financial decisions you make for the rest of your life, so opinion and sales hype should have no place in your financial plan.

We believe that financial decisions should be based on economic facts, and that all sales hype and opinions should be taken out of the equation. Because there is such a strong emotional attachment to money, this can be very difficult to do, especially if you are presented with information that is incongruent with what you have always thought to be true. A tremendous emotional disconnect is created when something that you always thought to be true is proven not to be. What we present may conflict with the "truths" to which you've been previously exposed. It can be difficult to admit that what you've been doing is not as good as you thought. Making a change means you have to overcome your emotional connection to money and develop the ability to separate facts from opinions.

This is why having a Financial Treatment Plan in your life is so important. Without this key piece as the foundation of your personal finances, it will be extremely difficult to remove emotions from financial decisions. When a Financial Treatment Plan is present in your life, you will have the ability to verify every financial decision based on economics and not sales hype or opinion. Let's examine the framework of the Financial Treatment Plan.

Our Financial Treatment Plan has three components: protection, savings, and growth. Each component has nine individual drawers for a total of twenty-seven drawers. These three components of protection, savings, and growth, as well as debt window and cash flow, are the framework for our game board of finance.

Every dentist develops individualized treatment plans for each patient. When the treatment plan is followed step by step, the end product will always be better than not following a plan. The same applies to our Financial Treatment Plan. When you follow the plan from the top (protection) to the bottom (growth), just as happens with a perfect treatment plan, the result will be a fantastic financial life.

The process is similar to evidence-based dentistry (EBD) where everything that dentists do on their treatment plan is based on science. If you believe in evidence-based dentistry, then how can you not believe in evidence-based financial planning? Ours is the only evidence-based Financial Treatment Plan of its kind.

Let's start with the protection component. The protection component is not where you accumulate wealth. Instead, it is where you protect your wealth so that it doesn't disappear overnight due to some unexpected situation. It is like the moat around a castle. The treasure or investments are held in the castle (savings and growth components) and the moat (protection component) keeps the marauders away.

Protection against unexpected events, such as a lawsuit, or onset of a disability or health issue, are essential. All of these events can and do occur in life; we just can't predict when. Thirty-one percent of orthodontists felt expenses from unexpected life events were a hindrance to being prepared for retirement.[9] If you were faced with any of these situations and had a chance to go back and purchase additional coverage to protect yourself, would you?

For example, if you were in a car accident in which you were clearly at fault, and you could be sued, how much coverage would you buy? You'd want maximum coverage, right? Or if you were disabled by an accident and could go back to the insurance company and add additional disability coverage backdated to the day before you were disabled, how much would you buy? Would you bother to ask about the cost of the premium or would you simply say you want maximum coverage?

With this in mind, if you know you'd want maximum coverage if such an event were to occur, shouldn't you own maximum coverage today even though you *don't know* if the event will occur? The answer is yes! Knowing this, what keeps most dentists from owning maximum protection today? The answer is simple. It is the perceived cost of the insurance premium.

With a Financial Treatment Plan, it is possible for dentists to acquire the protection coverage with little to no out-of-pocket cost to them by recovering expenses lost in the inefficiencies that are present in every traditional financial plan. Money that is already gushing out

---

9   Jeremiah Sturgill and Jae Park, "Changes in Orthodontists' Retirement Planning and Practice Operations Due to the Recent Recession."

of a financial plan can be redirected to carry the amount of coverage a dentist desires, and can do so with minimal to no additional outlay. If that can be done, would there be any reason why you wouldn't want to own maximum protection? Of course not!

The second component in the Financial Treatment Plan is savings. This is where a dentist's safe money resides in the Financial Treatment Plan. Safe money includes, for the most part, both liquid and retirement assets. Liquid assets are comprised of checking, savings, credit union accounts, US savings bonds, CDs, and money market accounts. A dentist's retirement accounts are also included in the savings component and have available the potential tax benefits of tax-deferral, tax-free, and tax-deductible investments. The tax benefits of a retirement account make these accounts the most powerful assets in the savings component.

It is an important to note that retirement plans are positioned in the savings section of the Financial Treatment Plan where safe money resides. Why? Because it is imperative that these funds are still around at the dentist's retirement age. As silly as this may sound, it is critical that retirement funds are invested more conservatively than nonretirement investments. We can't tell you all the horror stories we heard during the market crash of 2008, when retirement funds were invested too aggressively. As a result, when the market crashed, many dentists lost hundreds of thousands to millions of dollars unnecessarily! Since the lion's share of a dentist's total assets for retirement in traditional planning is a combination of 401(k)s and other retirement accounts, a lot of unnecessary pressure is placed on these accounts to perform from a rate-of-return standpoint. As a result, too much risk is assumed in these plans.

Saving provides you with freedom. At the beginning of our career we are all people at work with no money at work. By the end of our career, we want to have all our money at work and no people at work. This objective is only accomplished if we establish discipline in our saving habits.

• • • • • • • • • • • • • • • • • • • •

Mart

If you do not save money, you will *always* have to work. Savings is the fuel that drives a person's Financial Treatment Plan. It is like owning a car. If you want to go anywhere, you first have to put gas in it.

• • • • • • • • • • • • • • • • • • • •

The last component of the Financial Treatment Plan is the growth component. This is where our risk money resides. In this component, the word *safety* is replaced with the word *potential*. The growth component has the potential to deliver income, growth, and tax benefits, but there are no guarantees. Investing is exciting, but it is also risky.

The first layer of the growth component is where we become lenders of our money. We are, basically, lending money to governmental agencies, corporations, or municipalities in the form of a bond. We give them our money when we purchase a bond, and in return, they pay us a stated rate of interest. Our money is returned to us when we either sell the bond or it matures. It sounds safe enough, but there are inherent risks such as credit risk, interest rate risk, and default risk that we need to be aware of, especially in retirement when retirees tend to gravitate toward bonds in their asset allocation.

The second layer of the growth component is where we become investors in corporate America in the form of stock or equity ownership. We can invest in preferred stocks, blue chip stocks, mutual funds, exchange-traded funds (ETFs), or growth stocks. Depending on the type of stock owned, there could be income and/or growth potential realized. Preferred stocks will, typically, have a low growth potential that is offset by their high income potential from dividends paid. On the other end of the spectrum, growth stocks have minimal to zero income potential from dividends paid, but a high growth potential. We like to believe our stock investments will always appreciate in value, but that is not always the case, as we have all experienced!

The third layer of the growth component is where our hard assets are found. This is the highest risk portion of the entire model. Certainly there is potential for high returns, but there is also potential for total loss. Gold, silver, and collections such as art, stamps, or even comic books are considered hard assets. Bitcoin and cryptocurrencies reside in this layer of the Financial Treatment Plan as well, due to their extreme volatility and potential for gain and loss. Other assets in this layer could be a hobby that turns into a business, such as buying and selling antiques or a home business. Real estate is another powerful hard asset. It includes assets such as your personal residence, second home, office building where you practice, and rental property. Finally, the last component of the third layer is tax shelters, such as your dental practice, private equity investments, or captive insurance companies. Your practice is one of the most powerful assets you will own, but it holds a great deal of risk. As a small business owner, Uncle Sam gives you the opportunity to take advantage of some great tax benefits for carrying that risk. Your dental practice is a powerful place to build wealth.

In each component of protection, savings, and growth, the first drawer is the least powerful asset. The last drawer of each component is the most powerful. For example, in the protection component, your car insurance is the least powerful protection asset while your life insurance is the most powerful. In the savings component, your checking account is the least powerful, and the most powerful savings asset is your 401(k) or retirement plan. When you reach the growth component, government bonds are the least powerful and your practice is the most powerful. There is a hierarchy to the model and every insurance and investment product has a specific power and benefit.

Anybody who has played a board game, whether Monopoly, chess, or checkers, knows you have to have a set of rules to go along with the game board in order to play the game. If we just laid out a Monopoly board without the rules, nobody would be able to play. When a set of rules is introduced, however, people understand how to play Monopoly. The same goes for money. To be successful you have to have a game board such as a Financial Treatment Plan and a set of rules that are based on economics. These rules will be explained in chapter 5!

The key to a home standing the test of time is for the home to be built on a solid foundation first and foremost. This is no different when it comes to one's personal finances where the foundation is comprised of a rock-solid protection component. Without this in place your personal finances can and will crumble at some point. Once the protection component is established, the building blocks of the savings and growth components are added to build a Financial Treatment Plan for success. The integration and coordination of these three components, along with the debt window and cash flow, will ensure that your Financial Treatment Plan never develops a crack.

A Financial Treatment Plan built in this manner will provide total peace of mind knowing that, no matter what happens, life is going to be fantastic.

Every financial decision we make has benefits and disadvantages associated with it. As such, they all have to be considered for any financial decision to be properly evaluated. We are not saying that other advisors should not be a part of your financial team, but you need to have a macroadvisor involved to ensure that all of your advisors are on the same page and moving together in the right direction.

A statement we often hear in the dental world, and elsewhere, is that nobody is going to care more about your money than you. We believe this as well. All dentists should be actively engaged with their finances. If dentists try to manage their finances on their own, however, they may run into trouble, due to a lack of knowledge or the time and devotion that managing personal finances effectively requires. Also, dentists acting on their own behalf will certainly not have the Financial Treatment Plan, an essential tool for looking at their entire financial picture. They might be able to function as their own investment advisors, but it may be at the expense of a number of factors in their financial lives that they won't be aware of until it is too late.

Again, there is *no magic product* in the financial arena. We work with the exact same products that everybody else possesses. What is different about our approach is that we focus on the strategy behind the products versus the products themselves. It is the marriage (coordination and integration) of products within the Financial Treatment Plan that creates financial success. That's our winning strategy.

In the end, those dentists who don't have a Financial Treatment Plan create a junk drawer of inefficiency by purchasing products on an as-needed basis. When they are ready to retire, they are left with a bunch of products that are not integrated or coordinated with one another. This disorganization delivers a retirement income that is significantly less than their working income. On the other hand, when you have a *process* that is driven by a Financial Treatment Plan, you can build your retirement to ensure that you will have full income replacement. This means you take no pay cut in your golden years! The time to start your Financial Treatment Plan is *now*, but making that financial journey with a trusted Kemo Sabe at your side is essential!

Chapter 4

MONEY MYTHS DEBUNKED

• • •

*Reverse every natural instinct and do the opposite
of what you are inclined to do, and you will probably
come very close to having a perfect golf swing.*

—BEN HOGAN

Ben Hogan's advice on reversing "every natural instinct" if you want a successful golf swing can also be applied to financial planning. Do the opposite of what most people recommend and you will come very close to having a perfect financial life. When it comes to financial planning, most of the information available is actually misinformation. The traditional rules of thumb will lead to income insecurity.

Over the years, the rainmakers and their persistent messaging have penetrated our minds to the point that we can't even recognize the difference between financial misinformation and economic truth. The brainwashing of the American public by financial institutions and media runs deep! Nowhere is this brainwashing more prevalent than the promotion of what is touted as successful retirement planning. We always ask if this planning is so good, then why are the vast majority of Americans (78 percent) not prepared for retirement?[10] This statistic pertains to dentists as well, who, on average, retire with only 51 percent of their preretirement income, according to the most recent ADA study on retirement.[11]

Myth can be defined as a widely held but false belief or idea. People struggle financially due to the myths promoted by financial institutions. It is these myths that prevent dentists from becoming financially successful or having full income replacement at retirement. Even the savviest among us buy into these myths. Let's debunk four of the biggest money myths (keep in mind that there are many more).

THE MYTH OF DEBT REPAYMENT

There is a prevailing belief that *all* debt is bad. If you have *any* debt you need to get rid of it as fast as possible. Some pundits even compare debt to a sin. The truth is that not *all* debt is bad debt. There is debt that is good, and if it is managed properly, it can make you wealthier. Bad debt, however, does need to be addressed and understood.

Let's address the bad debt first. This type of debt has high interest rates or interest that is nondeductible. Consumer debt, such as credit card debt, is at the top of that list. You want to get rid of high interest debt as soon as possible. The best way to pay off those credit cards is in the following manner: Arrange your credit card balances from the highest to the lowest. Begin by taking any excess monthly cash flow that can be used for debt reduction and use it to pay off the lowest credit card balance first, regardless of the credit card's interest

10   The Data Driven Investor, December 14, 2018.

11   "2010 Survey on Retirement and Investment," American Dental Association.

rate. Once that card is paid off, apply that card's monthly payment (including the excess monthly cash flow) to the next lowest credit card balance until that card balance is paid off. Continue that process until all the credit cards are paid off. This strategy pays off credit card debt very quickly. Also, starting the process with credit cards that have the lowest balance gives you emotional momentum to continue chipping off the debt more quickly.

If you have car loans or other consumer debt with high interest rates, try and eliminate them as quickly as possible in the same manner. However, if you have a car note that carries a 0 percent or 1.9 percent interest rate, there is no reason to accelerate that debt repayment as those funds can be better used elsewhere. This is why it is important to look at each debt individually.

Contrary to what many of the radio pundits preach today, even in churches across America, there actually is such a thing as good debt. One type of good debt is a properly structured mortgage. The reason for this is twofold. First, mortgage interest is still one of the few tax deductions available (although the Tax Reform Act of 2018 somewhat lessened this deduction).

Second, you should also consider how inflation impacts a mortgage payment over time. Inflation is your friend when it comes to mortgage loans. Today is the only day that your dollar is worth 100 cents. As time goes on, inflation will dramatically decrease the value of that dollar. As an example, if you pay cash for your home today, in essence you have used dollars valued at 100 cents to pay off your mortgage. If you take a thirty-year mortgage out to purchase your home, you will purchase your home with 360 fixed monthly payments over thirty years. Every year you have that mortgage, you are paying the financial institution back with cheaper dollars due to the impact of inflation. At a 3 percent inflation rate, in the fifteenth year, you are using dollars worth only sixty-four cents to make your mortgage payment. At the end of thirty years, the dollars you use to pay the mortgage will only be worth forty-one cents!

Low interest rates also make mortgages attractive, especially when they are tax-deductible. It is almost like free money in a low-interest-rate environment. Even if mortgage rates are 5 percent, that is still a low rate.

When structuring your mortgage, you want a mortgage term that is fixed for as long as possible, such as thirty years, not fifteen years. Also, you definitely don't want an adjustable rate mortgage (ARM). That interest rate will adjust annually after a fixed interest rate period of five to seven years. An ARM in certain situations can work if the homeowner is going to be out of the house before the ARM reaches the end of its fixed term (e.g., the homeowner has a seven-year ARM and intends to stay in the home no longer than five years). When people intend to stay in their home for the long term, an ARM does not make a lot of sense, especially if interest rates are low. In this situation, you could expose yourself to higher interest rates when the mortgage adjusts, as you have no control over mortgage rates in the future.

An ARM mortgage can unnecessarily expose an individual to future interest rate risk. The term length of your debt should match the longevity of the asset being purchased. In the case of purchasing a home, a fixed-rate, thirty-year mortgage is most likely your best option.

With this information in mind, let's break down the three most common ways to pay for a home. In this example, we will examine the efficiency of either paying cash outright or using a fifteen- or thirty-year mortgage to acquire the residence. The facts related to this home purchase are:

Purchase price: $500,000

Down payment: 20 percent, or $100,000

Mortgage rate options: fifteen-year loan at 4.50 percent; thirty-year loan at 4.75 percent

Personal federal tax bracket: 30 percent

Cost of money (opportunity cost): 6 percent

Analysis period: 360 months (30 years)

The financial world we live in today promotes the idea that paying cash, or at the very least accelerating the repayment of a mortgage, is the best way to purchase a house. After all, if you were to pay cash for your home, no mortgage interest would be incurred. In contrast, if you have a thirty-year mortgage in this scenario, you would pay a whopping $351,172 of interest over thirty years. We have all been told that paying interest on debt is bad, and we should avoid it, or at the very least, find a way to minimize this expense. Most individuals don't have the cash reserves available to pay cash for a home, so the next best alternative for them, in order to avoid high interest costs, is to accept a fifteen-year mortgage instead. In this example, the interest costs for a fifteen-year mortgage are $150,795. See table 4.1 on the next page for a summary of these results.

MORTGAGE OPTIONS	DOWN PAYMENT	MORTGAGE PAYMENT	CUMULATIVE INTEREST
Cash	$500,000	-0-	-0-
15-year loan	$100,000	$3,060	$150,795
30-year loan	$100,000	$2,087	$351,172

Table 4.1

At this point, if we base our decision on how we pay for a home solely on the potential interest costs incurred, then paying cash or opting for a shorter-term mortgage makes all the sense in the world. A thirty-year mortgage would make no sense at all due to the higher interest costs.

This is the exact reasoning you will hear from traditional financial advisors, bankers, and the various financial entertainers advising you on the TV and radio, and in the print media. Their analysis of how you should pay for a home is based solely on interest costs incurred and does not look at the complete picture. There are other factors that have to be considered in looking at how you should pay for a home. The two biggest factors overlooked by traditional financial advisors are individual opportunity cost (cost of money) and the benefit of any tax savings generated from a potential mortgage-interest tax deduction.

Opportunity cost, which is never considered in the traditional world of planning, is a key concept in economics. The *New Oxford American Dictionary* defines opportunity cost as "the loss of potential gain from other alternatives when one alternative is chosen." In this case, every dollar used to purchase a home, including cash up front or the remittance of monthly mortgage payments over time, generates an opportunity cost as these dollars could have been used for an alternative investment. In our analysis, we have assigned an opportunity cost of 6 percent (see table 4.2).

MORTGAGE OPTIONS	(A) COMPOUNDED PRINCIPAL AND INTEREST	CUMULATIVE TAX SAVINGS	(B) COMPOUNDED TAX SAVINGS	(A–B) NET COMPOUND MORTGAGE COST
Cash	$3,011,288	-0-	-0-	$3,011,288
15-year loan	$2,786,149	$45,239	$202,625	$2,583,524
30-year loan	$2,698,268	$105,352	$356,842	$2,341,426

Table 4.2

The compounded principal and interest amount for a cash purchase in this example totals $3,011,288 after thirty years. This amount simply represents the original $500,000 cash payment for the house, invested at 6 percent over thirty years in an alternative investment. The most cost-effective way to purchase the home was accomplished with a thirty-year mortgage. The compounded principal and interest amount of $2,698,268 represents a 6 percent alternative investment in which an initial deposit of $100,000 and 360 monthly contributions of $2,087 were made.

Another factor that comes into play is the potential mortgage-interest tax deduction on the loan. The cumulative tax savings generated from this tax deduction and the related opportunity costs must be measured and netted out of the compound mortgage loan cost as well. When all economic factors are measured macroeconomically, it is rare that anything less than a thirty-year mortgage makes sense.

• • • • • • • • • • • • • • • • • • • •

Mart

We have found in almost every client situation that a thirty-year mortgage is the most cost effective way to purchase a home. Having a thirty-year mortgage does not mean that it cannot be paid off in a shorter period of time if that makes sense. Finally, it is important to remember that a home appreciates at the same rate whether the property has a mortgage against it or not.

• • • • • • • • • • • • • • • • • • • •

• • • • • • • • • • • • • • • • • • • •

Tim

Another way to think of this mortgage dilemma is to examine the situation of two dentists. Dentist A has a half-million-dollar home that is free and clear with no other assets or debt. This means his net worth is $500,000. Dentist B also has a net worth of $500,000, comprised of a half-million-dollar home with a $250,000 mortgage and cash of $250,000 ($500,000 home + $250,000 cash minus $250,000 mortgage = $500,000).

Which dentist would you rather be? Dentist A, who has a debt-free home and zero cash in his model, or Dentist

B, who has a $500,000 home with a $250,000 mortgage and $250,000 in cash?

Could Dentist B pay off his mortgage tomorrow and be in the exact same position as Dentist A? Of course, he could. So, in reality, Dentist B is debt-free but with more wealth-building options. For example, if the interest rate environment is one where CD rates are paying 10–12 percent (as in the early 1980s, see Bankrate.com), and Dentist B has a mortgage locked in at 4 percent, why would he use his cash to pay off his mortgage when he could invest it in a CD and earn substantially more interest? In this situation, as emotionally satisfying as it may be to be debt-free, nobody who wants to be wealthier would pay off the mortgage and possibly lose the tax deduction if a safe CD could more than triple that cash. Not even a radio personality would do this!

Now some of you may be thinking that Dentist A could also do the same thing by pulling money out of his home via a new mortgage or home equity line of credit (HELOC) to invest in the CD. That could certainly be done, but if CD rates are at 10 percent, you can be certain that interest rates for a new mortgage, or HELOC, will be higher as well. Would you pull money out of your home at 12 percent to invest it in a 10 percent CD? This does not make sense, even though a 10 percent CD is fantastic. What this comes down to is that those who win have more control of their cash.

The point is that cash flow is king. Whoever has the cash gets to make the rules and is in control. If you do not have control of your cash, you are subject to the whims of others.

• • • • • • • • • • • • • • • • • • • •

Some of our initial principles in the Financial Treatment Plan are aimed at getting your annual savings rate up to 15 percent or more and building a liquidity position equal to 50 percent of one year's gross household income. If you are focused solely on eliminating all of your debt before you do anything else, it will take significantly longer to have that liquidity in place, a move that would be financially dangerous. If you're throwing everything you have into paying off your debt, you'll be in trouble if a situation were to arise that demands funds and you have no liquidity to address that situation. You're paying off debt at the expense of liquidity.

When you throw all of your excess cash flow into debt reduction, you forgo other opportunities that may provide you with better investment returns and benefits. In the end, improperly paying off debt means fewer income streams in retirement as well, which usually means you will be working longer. This is why it is financially unhealthy to focus on debt repayment from a linear viewpoint (microviewpoint), as it will make you poorer.

For instance, if you pay off your house in ten years, you may think you've made a great decision. After all, this is what your traditional advisors or parents have advised you to do. You may be thinking that you will be mortgage-free in ten years and will have saved thousands of dollars in mortgage interest over a thirty-year mortgage. However, macroeconomically, it could be the wrong decision because the monies that went toward that mortgage repayment might have been better used elsewhere, as, for example, in investments or insurance. Also, and maybe more importantly, what other benefits did you give up by prematurely locking your money up in the equity of your home?

Another good debt is a student loan. As a dentist, you might not have been able to pursue your career without incurring that debt. Student loan debt is an *investment*, not a *cost*. It's an investment in your career, but it needs to be managed properly. You want your loan terms fixed and you want to be in control of it. Some student loan repayments are based on a dentist's income, which frequently makes the loan a negative amortizing note. This means that even though you are making payments, the loan balance is still going up. That's a future train wreck. It is imperative that dentists amortize student loans as quickly as possible upon graduation. Also, for cash flow purposes, larger loans should, initially, be amortized for as long as possible.

We acknowledge this is a different way of looking at debt, but quite frankly, you must have the training and the degree to practice as a dentist and earn a lot of money. That degree is going to allow you to earn hundreds of thousands of dollars a year. If you come out of school with a debt of $200,000–300,000 or more, that is your buy-in to a career that will deliver substantial income to you over your lifetime.

● ● ● ● ● ● ● ● ● ● ● ● ● ● ● ● ● ● ●

Tim

If you were able to start contributing $50,000 a year to your 401(k) plan at age thirty and you continued doing this for the next thirty-five years, at a 6 percent rate of return, you would have accumulated $5.9 million by age sixty-five. If you were, instead, to delay your $50,000 contribution to a 401(k) plan by ten years (and begin contributing at age forty) because you were initially concentrating on paying off your debt, then, at age sixty-five, you would have only $2.9 million at a 6 percent rate of return. You lost three million dollars of potential wealth because you were focused solely on eliminating debt, directing excess cash flow to that objective before starting a retirement plan.

I am totally on board with getting rid of consumer debt and high-interest credit-card debt, but to make a blanket statement that all debt has to be eliminated is shooting yourself in the foot.

• • • • • • • • • • • • • • • • • • • •

In conclusion, if you can amortize your good loans at a low interest rate, receive a tax deduction, and let inflation be your friend over time, you will realize the double benefit of maintaining control *and* flexibility of your money over the course of your loan.

THE MYTH OF FUNDING THE RETIREMENT PLAN TO THE MAXIMUM

All our new clients have been advised by their accountant or financial advisor to fund their retirement plan at the maximum level if they want to have a successful retirement. Typically, the recommendation is a 401(k) safe harbor plan that includes a profit-sharing contribution. This means that, for most dentists, the majority of their savings are going into a retirement plan. As with all financial products, however, 401(k) plans have advantages and disadvantages that need to be evaluated.

A fallacy that is often repeated in traditional financial planning circles is that contributors to a tax-deductible retirement plan such as a 401(k) are saving taxes. There are *no* tax savings on this contribution! Instead, contributors only receive a tax deduction for their contribution today with a tax deferral on future growth. In the future, ordinary income taxes will be paid on withdrawals. As a result, there is an embedded tax in every tax-deductible retirement plan. The only way you will receive a tax savings from such a plan is if you happen to be in a lower tax bracket when you retire. If this occurs, due to taking a pay cut in retirement, then your advisor has failed you because you will have less income to enjoy in your golden years.

When dentists fill out a balance sheet for their lenders or themselves, they list their checking, savings, investments, and retirement plans as assets. When they list their liabilities, however, they never itemize the corresponding tax liability that is due on their retirement plan. As a result, every personal balance sheet is overstated from a net worth standpoint.

Dentists never take this into account until it is brought to their attention. The Securities and Exchange Commission (SEC) would never allow a business to only list the value of their assets and not state their corresponding liabilities, whether current or deferred, yet it is accepted in the personal finance arena. With this in mind, most personal financial statements are not accurate.

Although the payment of this embedded tax in the retirement plan is deferred to some unknown point in the future, it is still a real cost that must be recognized. Keep in mind that the cost of this deferred tax will increase if, at the time of withdrawal, you are in a higher tax bracket than the tax bracket you were in at the time of your original deferral rate. You will pay that tax at some point in time and tax rates have continuously changed throughout history (see the following

Bradford Tax Institute graph). The compounding that occurs as part of a retirement plan may not generate the same compound tax impact that occurs in an after-tax investment during growth years, but it is not free. You will pay that tax later in life. There is no free lunch!

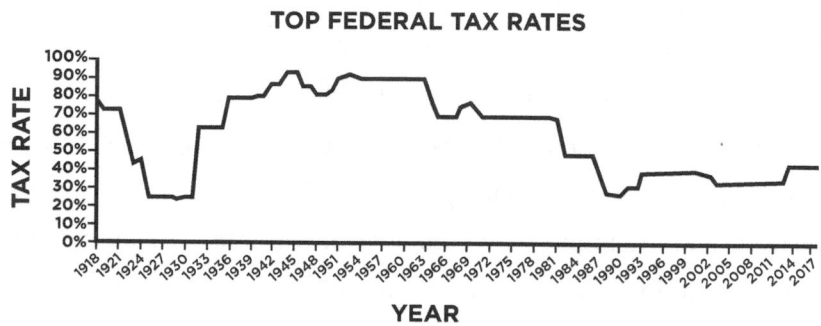

Bradford Tax Institute Graph

Figure 4.1

There are positive things about a traditional retirement plan. The money goes in before tax and it grows, tax-deferred, until you withdraw it at retirement. There are also some negative things that must be considered. The biggest negative issue is that once your money goes in, under present tax laws, it is locked up until you are at least the age of fifty-nine and a half. If you take money out before then, you will pay a 10 percent premature distribution penalty, plus ordinary income taxes on the money at that time. Accessing your own money from a retirement plan prior to the age of fifty-nine and a half is very costly. There is a way for limited access to these funds without penalty prior to age fifty-nine and a half, but you must follow very specific IRS guidelines to accomplish this.

Another drawback to having money in a retirement plan is that you have no control over these assets other than where you may invest them. It is important to keep in mind who is responsible for making all of the rules for retirement plans. In this instance, the rainmaker is the federal government. The government tells us how much money we can put into our retirement plans and when we can take funds out. It also dictates the tax rate we will pay at the time of withdrawal. Unfortunately, this rate is subject to change as tax laws are revised with each newly elected congress.

Another huge consideration that is never discussed when making a retirement contribution is the fact that government can change the age of withdrawal. Let's assume that you want to retire at age sixty, which many dentists do. You may get within two years of retirement and the government could change the withdrawal age to sixty-five or sixty-seven. How excited would you be about your money sitting in a retirement plan, knowing that you will have to work longer in order to get the money out penalty-free? If you think that can't happen, think again. There has already been talk of extending the withdrawal age to as late as age seventy. If this actually came to pass, would that affect how you would save for retirement?

● ● ● ● ● ● ● ● ● ● ● ● ● ● ● ● ● ● ●

Tim

Years ago you could access money held in a retirement plan at any age without penalty. Since then, the government has implemented a minimum age requirement of fifty-nine and a half for withdrawal, which an investor must adhere to in order to avoid an early withdrawal penalty. My point is this: the government is always looking for ways to force people to work for a longer period of time, not a shorter one. This statement is also supported by the fact that the government has gradually extended the age to receive full Social Security benefits to age sixty-seven for those born in 1960 or later. They also further reduced the Social Security benefits for those retiring as early as age sixty-two. I believe that the government fully recognizes the fact that their tax revenue base relies more on working people than retired people.

• • • • • • • • • • • • • • • • • • • •

When we look at retirement, we include everything in the Financial Treatment Plan, not just a 401(k) plan, which is only one drawer of the model. Why can't your retirement plan include a 401(k) plan as well as other assets such as after-tax investments, municipal bonds, income-producing real estate, and a business that you build and sell? Your retirement plan should include all of these things and more, not just a 401(k).

Dentists, typically, have three buckets from which to pull income during retirement: Social Security, their 401(k), and the sale of their practice. The 401(k) is the primary investment vehicle for 60 percent of orthodontists.[12] When the *whole* Financial Treatment Plan is used as the retirement plan, rather than being limited to these three buckets, dentists have the opportunity to add another five to eight income streams in retirement. Having multiple income streams in retirement adds diversification to the overall retirement income and retirees are no longer dependent on any one income source, which adds peace of mind to their retirement. As was mentioned earlier, successful Americans have at least seven income streams in retirement, and you should too. We call this diversifying your income streams.

---

12   Jeremiah Sturgill and Jae Park, "Changes in Orthodontists' Retirement Planning and Practice Operations Due to the Recent Recession."

Recall our earlier example of contributing $50,000 to a 401(k) for thirty-five years at 6 percent to generate $5.9 million by retirement. Many dentists look at that number and think, *Great! My retirement is done.* The problem is, however, no matter how big the final number, every financial decision has a cost. A retirement plan is no different. These costs may not be fully disclosed, but they still exist. When we look at a 401(k) plan or a profit-sharing plan, there are always embedded costs.

• • • • • • • • • • • • • • • • • • •

Mart

Dentist A is setting up a 401(k) plan. In order for Dentist A to fully participate in the 401(k), she will have to provide a safe harbor match for her employees. This match will oftentimes range from 3 to 4 percent of their wages. Assuming staff wages of $250,000 and a 4 percent match, this amounts to a $10,000 employer contribution that Dentist A will make each year. Now, this match may be viewed by the staff as a great employee benefit and may, ultimately, be an incentive for employees to remain with Dentist A's practice long-term. Nonetheless, we have to recognize the match as an annual cost to Dentist A's practice.

In addition, there are administrative fees associated with the 401(k) plan. Typically, they will run anywhere from $4,000 to $5,000 a year. Assuming Dentist A contributes a match of $10,000 plus administrative fees of $4,000, Dentist A's annual costs for the 401(k) plan are $14,000 each year. Over twenty-five years, her total out-of-pocket costs will amount to $350,000. If a discretionary profit-sharing contribution is made each year in order for Dentist A to fully maximize her contribution to the 401(k), these costs are only increased. They could easily exceed well over a half a million dollars, in total, over time.

No matter how much money Dentist A makes, this is a lot of money! Unfortunately, this is only part of the story when it comes to plan costs; there is also an opportunity cost on the $14,000 paid annually for the 401(k) plan. If these monies were not paid out and instead retained in Dentist A's Financial Treatment Plan, they could have been invested for her benefit. For example, if she had invested the annual costs of $14,000 at 6 percent over twenty-five years, they would have grown to be $814,000. This is the real cost of sponsoring a 401(k) plan, and it must be considered when looking at a 401(k) plan.

Again, we are not saying that a 401(k) should not be part of a dentist's overall retirement strategy. After all, according to our economic rules of wealth building (discussed in the next chapter), it should be. Thus a 401(k) has a place in overall wealth building. However, we encourage dentists not to simply fall in line with the rest of the herd, who are being led over a cliff by the traditional financial world. Financial advisors who indiscriminately promote to dentists the full funding of a safe harbor 401(k) plan at more than $50,000 annually (or worse yet, a cash balance plan that may allow a dentist to add upward of $200,000 or more to retirement accounts) do great harm. These plans have real costs, which you need to know before committing to sponsoring a 401(k). Once plan costs are identified, it's important to look at how those costs can be minimized or, better yet, recaptured over time.

• • • • • • • • • • • • • • • • • • •

Let's look at another piece of traditional retirement advice, which involves putting your spouse on the payroll with a salary of more than $25,000 a year. This is oftentimes recommended for the sole purpose of allowing the spouse to make a maximum contribution of $19,000 (for those under the age of fifty) to a 401(k) plan. Again, more money going into the 401(k) will make the retirement numbers look bigger in the end, but at what cost? By placing a spouse on the payroll, the dentist has taken income that may have been distributed to the family as unearned income via a bonus or distribution and turned it into earned income, which is now subject to FICA payroll taxes of 15.3 percent. The FICA payroll taxes on a salary of $25,000 are $3,825. These additional payroll taxes literally represent what is, in essence, a 20 percent front-end load (charge) in order for your spouse to put $19,000 into a 401(k) plan.

Stop and think about it. If we said, "We've got a great investment that allows you to contribute $19,000 each year to an account, but it has a front-end load of 20 percent," how excited would you be to put money into that investment? We are fairly certain that you wouldn't do it. Yet, for spouses who are on the payroll for the sole purpose of making a retirement contribution, this is an annual front-end load as FICA taxes are paid on the spouse's salary every year!

Instead of placing your spouse on the payroll, and incurring a cost of almost $24,000 (consisting of the 401(k) contribution of

$19,000, a safe harbor match, and the FICA taxes paid of $3,825), consider buying a second home. Use the $24,000 ($2,000 per month) to pay toward the monthly mortgage on a second home. Now you can actually live in your 401(k), so to speak, and create lasting memories with your family and friends today. What is the rate of return on enjoyment when creating memories with your family? We actually believe that it can't be measured, as it is infinite. Most certainly it is far greater than any paper return on a retirement plan that will provide you no enjoyment until you retire. Also keep in mind that the appreciation on the real estate is taxed at capital gain rates, whereas the gains in a retirement plan are taxed as ordinary income when withdrawn from the plan.

As mentioned in chapter 2, the ownership of a second home may provide additional tax deductions in the form of mortgage interest and real estate taxes paid. These deductions were limited, however, with the passing of the Tax Cuts and Jobs Act of 2017. Also, depending on the property's location, it could become an income-producing rental property when the family is not using it. Another benefit of renting out the property is that you can deduct any expenses for the property maintenance and upkeep. (Please consult an accountant for all tax deductions.)

Financial institutions, corporations, and the government promulgate the traditional money myths we cling to. It goes back to the three entities, or rainmakers, we identified earlier that are fighting for our money. Almost twenty-five trillion dollars are held in retirement funds in America today.[13] The financial institutions are managing these monies and charging fund fees, management fees, and advisory

---

13   Nick Thornton, "Total retirement assets near $25 trillion mark," Benefits PRO, June 30, 2015, https://www.benefitspro.com/2015/06/30/total-retirement-assets-near-25-trillion-mark.

fees. Is it to their benefit to discourage people from contributing to these plans? Also, do they encourage people to withdraw money from their retirement accounts to spend and enjoy? The answer is no, because that diminishes the fee income these financial institutions receive each year.

Instead, they tell us to throw all of our money into retirement accounts so that we can retire. When we get to retirement age, they tell us that "to avoid a big tax burden on any money withdrawn from the account, you should defer withdrawals from the retirement plan until seventy and a half years old." When we reach age seventy and a half, we are then told that in order to further avoid or minimize taxes, we should only take out the required minimum distribution (RMD), which starts at about 3.6 percent of the account balance. Well, that's great! You poured all this money into a retirement plan during your working years only to continue deferring it when you initially retire. Then when you do finally take distributions from your retirement plan at seventy and a half, you set yourself up to take minimum distributions from the plan. Why would you not want to have maximum distributions from your retirement plan from day one of retirement? In the traditional world, if you only take RMD distributions from your retirement plan, you may very well decrease your tax burden, but you will most certainly reduce your enjoyment of life in retirement.

• • • • • • • • • • • • • • • • • • • •

Mart

There are large dental advisory firms across the country that charge dentists an annual fee of $5,000 to $25,000 *per year* for planning services. If the dental advisory firm also manages investments for their clients, then those clients will also pay investment fees to that firm. In this case, a dentist is actually paying double for the firm's services. These advisors cost their clients millions of dollars of lost wealth through these additional and unnecessary fees. Dentists often think they're getting great advice because they're paying a planning fee. That money, however, is pulled from the dentist's pockets never to return. Instead, the money is enriching the advisor at the expense of the dentist.

• • • • • • • • • • • • • • • • • • • •

As if the costs to have a retirement plan were not bad enough already, let's analyze the impact of investment advisory fees that are paid out to financial advisors. Again, back to the example where we talked about saving $50,000 into a retirement plan for thirty-five years. If we assume a 1 percent advisory fee over thirty-five years, the advisor will collect $593,000 in fees over those thirty-five years. Because these fees are netted out of the account results (*netting* means "taking the fees from the account directly"), your account balance at age sixty-five will approximate $4.7 million and not the $5.9 million originally projected. You want to talk about wealth erosion? That 1 percent advisory fee just cost you $1.2 million in terms of the accumulation value of your account.

Unfortunately, most people are paying an investment advisory fee that is greater than 1 percent. This is eye opening to say the least. Fees have to be paid to the advisor, but it is essential to keep them as low as possible. Better yet, the advisor should build cost recovery strategies into the Financial Treatment Plan to fully recover these fees. This is ideal planning!

We want you to learn to focus on obtaining multiple uses of the same dollar, rather than only getting a singular use from each dollar over your lifetime. Money that goes into a retirement plan counts as one use for that dollar. Once that dollar is in that plan, it's trapped until you are at least age fifty-nine and a half. If you're going to put money into a retirement plan, why not run it through another area of your Financial Treatment Plan first so that by the time that dollar goes into your retirement plan, you will be getting a second or third use from it? That way you get two or three uses out of the same dollar and create additional benefits and money supply before that dollar is locked up in a retirement account.

A final thought on retirement plans is from a tax and estate planning perspective. Do you really want to die with all your money stuck in a retirement plan that only benefits and enriches the financial institutions? The answer to this question should be an unequivocal no. Funds left in a retirement plan at death may be subject to huge tax consequences. Also, keep in mind that tax laws change and will continue to do so. When everything is considered, we often find that dentists' retirement funds should be spent first (not last) so they can fully enjoy their money while they are alive.

The decision to fund a retirement plan is an important one, but understanding the many moving parts of these plans has a significant impact on your future retirement income. A lack of understanding will result in less income in your golden years. Knowing the advantages and disadvantages of these plans will position you for full income replacement in retirement!

THE MYTH OF TERM LIFE INSURANCE

Of all the insurance coverage we purchase throughout our lifetime, there is only one that we are guaranteed to use and that is life insurance! Why? Because we are mortal and dying is a natural part of life. Since dying is guaranteed, doesn't it make sense to have it until that time? This may sound like common sense, yet very few people have life insurance in force when they die.

Let's start here: Term life insurance is a product no one uses. If you qualify for term insurance today, the chances of your loved ones collecting a death benefit on that policy are less than 1 percent.[14] Yes, less than 1 percent! Why? Because term life insurance is priced to expire before *you* expire.

Through the life underwriting process, life insurance companies can determine with great accuracy your life expectancy. Unexpected events or accidents aside, the insured will outlive their term insurance 99 percent of the time. As a result, most people pay term premiums to an insurance company for a policy that will never pay a death benefit, due to the fact that the term policy either expired or has been dropped long before the person dies. This is what makes it such a great product for insurance companies. It is the most profitable form of life insurance that an insurance company can sell. Wouldn't it be great to sell an insurance product in which there is less than a 1 percent chance of ever having to pay a claim? The sale of term life insurance is a license to print money for the insurance companies.

---

14   Doug Mitchell, "Why Term Life Insurance Is Cheaper," BestLifequote, February 12, 2019, https://www.bestlifequote.com/blog/cheap-term-life-insurance.

(On a side note, the least profitable form of life insurance sold is whole life insurance.)

Every advisor, including us, will tell you that you should have some form of life insurance. Term life insurance, on the surface, appears to be the most cost-effective way to purchase life insurance. From a macroeconomic standpoint, however, it's the most expensive form of life insurance a person will ever own. The reason for this is that the cost of term insurance *never* ends!

People are led to believe that the cost of term insurance is limited to the total premiums paid and that the costs stop when the policy is canceled. The true total cost of term insurance is threefold: it includes 1) the total premiums paid over the insured's lifetime, plus 2) the opportunity costs on the term premiums paid until the insured's death, and 3) ultimately, the lost death benefit that is never paid out at death to a surviving spouse, children, and future generations. The true cost of term insurance to families will total hundreds of thousands and oftentimes millions of dollars over the insured's lifetime. Let's look at a common example:

Insured's current age: thirty-five

Age at death: eighty-five

Death benefit: $1,000,000

Level term period: thirty years

Annual premium: $700

Cost of money (opportunity cost): 6 percent

The traditional financial world has trained us to view the cost of term insurance as only the total amount of premiums paid. In this example, if we had a thirty-year level term policy with an annual premium of $700, our total cost for the term would be $21,000 over thirty years. At the end of thirty years, the premium would cease and the death benefit of $1,000,000 would go away.

In reality, though, the premiums paid could have been invested and earned interest. At a 6 percent opportunity cost, the premiums paid over thirty years would have grown to $58,661 if invested instead. This is a significant cost with no ultimate benefit as the death benefit is completely lost at the end of the level term period.

**OPPORTUNITY COST OF
30-YEAR TERM INSURANCE**

Annual payment: $700

Interest rate: 6 percent

Number of years: 30

FUTURE VALUE: $58,661

Unfortunately, the cost of the term will not cease just because you stop paying premiums. The expense of $58,661 for lost premiums and interest at the end of thirty years will continue to accrue lost earnings for the rest of that individual's lifetime. If this person were to live another twenty years to age eighty-five, the total cost of premiums paid and lost earnings would amount to $188,134. This lost wealth was, essentially, transferred to the insurance company as it collected premiums over thirty years, invested those profits, and ultimately, never had to pay a death benefit.

> **OPPORTUNITY COST BEYOND 30-YEAR TERM INSURANCE**
>
> Present value: $58,661
>
> Interest rate: 6 percent
>
> Number of years: 20
>
> FUTURE VALUE: $188,134

The loss of the death benefit at death is the largest cost to the individual. In our example above, that was an additional $1,000,000 on top of the $188,134 for a total of $1,188,134 of lost wealth to a spouse, loved ones, or charity. Upon full analysis, term life insurance is by far the most expensive life insurance anyone could ever own.

The financial entertainers tell us to buy term and invest the difference. After all, term insurance is cheap. People can take the amount they save (the difference in premium costs between a term and permanent insurance policy) and invest it in the stock market. At first glance, this strategy seems to make sense, but from a macroeconomic standpoint it is financially devastating. As David Babbel, professor at the Wharton School of the University of Pennsylvania, wrote, "People don't buy term and invest the difference."[15] This strategy is a recipe for a guaranteed pay cut in retirement and a sig-

---

15   David F. Babbel and Oliver D. Hahl, "Buy Term and Invest the Difference Revisited," *Journal of Financial Service Professionals* 69, no. 3 (May 2015): https://www.academia.edu/31450051/Buy_Term_and_Invest_the_Difference_Revisited.

nificant loss of wealth for your family and the charities to which you might contribute in the future!

Term insurance can be benign or malignant due to its substantial wealth-eroding nature. Financial charlatans do not delineate between the two types of term insurance, yet understanding this difference can be the difference for you between the retirement of your dreams or one that is shrouded in financial uncertainty.

What is the difference between term life insurance that is diagnosed as malignant versus one diagnosed as benign? Early in dentists' careers, when resources are scarce and they still want the security of life insurance coverage, term insurance is appropriate as a short-term solution. If term insurance is carried throughout a dentist's career as a long-term strategy, it becomes very costly to own, as we just demonstrated in our example.

Term insurance that is owned in this manner is malignant and deadly to the dentist's long-term financial well-being. In order for term insurance to remain in a benign state, it must be eliminated from a dentist's Financial Treatment Plan as soon as possible. Often-times this is accomplished by converting the term insurance to a whole life policy. A key provision of a term policy is its conversion option. If term is purchased, it is important that you confirm that the policy has a conversion option to a whole life policy that allows the insured to convert from a term to a whole life policy in the future regardless of their health at the time. Eliminating the benign tumor, or term insurance, sooner than later prevents the term insurance from becoming malignant. Permanent insurance is all about living, while term insurance is only about dying. The last time we checked, dying is not a desired benefit for anyone.

As you age, and get closer to your mortality date, term insurance becomes much more expensive. Term insurance is often written in level term periods ranging from ten to thirty years. You will pay the least amount for a ten-year contract, while a thirty-year contract is the most expensive. For all the reasons illustrated in our example, a thirty-year policy is the most harmful.

If you are fortunate enough to live to the end of your level term period, your initial premium will then skyrocket, if you wish to keep the coverage. When you realize that your premium will rise substantially, you will drop the coverage. At that time, the premiums paid over the years, as well as the death benefit, are lost forever. It is like taking a million dollars off of your balance sheet and flushing it down the toilet. There is no way, unless you happen to die early, to benefit from term life insurance.

A death benefit that is guaranteed to remain in force until the day you die, is a turbocharger to your Financial Treatment Plan and a huge difference maker to your retirement. Owning permanent life insurance strategically positioned in your Financial Treatment Plan (discussed later in the book) will essentially allow you to spend your death benefit while you are alive. This will provide you with greater guaranteed income in retirement and allow you to pass your death benefit on when you die! Term insurance can have a place in your life as a short-term solution, but the long-term solution is permanent coverage.

THE MYTH OF COMPOUND INTEREST

A sacred principle in the traditional world of personal finance is compound interest. We have heard it called the million-dollar secret and it is commonly referred to as the eighth wonder of the world. The eighth wonder comparison has been attributed to Einstein (although there is no verification of this). However, being a nuclear physicist, it is likely that he was speaking of compounding numbers, and not interest or money. We think that economists, and even Einstein, would say that there is a big difference between math and money. Robert Castiglione coined the brilliant phrase, "Math is not money and money is not math."

One of the biggest drawbacks to compounding interest in any investment is the fact that when you compound interest back into an account, you only receive one use of that dollar. When interest earned simply goes back into an account, it is not seizing the opportunity to create a new asset or taking advantage of additional benefits within the Financial Treatment Plan. Compounding interest in a taxable account creates another problem: taxes must be paid on the interest, dividends, or capital gains earned by the account. These additional taxes are a real cost to the investment and must be considered when evaluating an investment decision. Let's examine a compound interest scenario and its overall impact on a dentist's financial well-being.

In this scenario, the dentist has invested $100,000 in an after-tax investment that is yielding 5 percent. The investment time frame covers a thirty-year time period and the dentist's tax bracket is 30 percent. Also, on the recommendation of the dentist's financial planner, the dentist will reinvest the annual interest earned on the investment in the account (see Figure 4.2 on the next page for a visual of this scenario).

TRADITIONAL COMPOUNDING

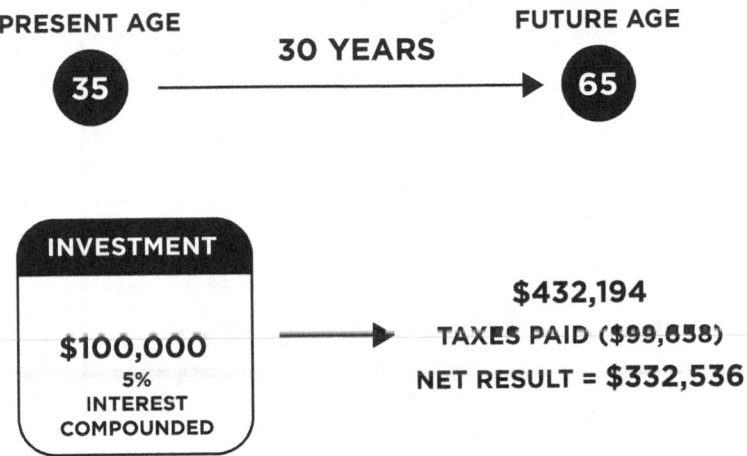

PRESENT AGE

35

30 YEARS

FUTURE AGE

65

INVESTMENT

$100,000
5%
INTEREST
COMPOUNDED

$432,194
TAXES PAID ($99,658)
NET RESULT = $332,536

ASSUMPTIONS
MARGINAL TAX BRACKET: 30%

Figure 4.2

At the end of thirty years the investment account will have grown to $432,194 due to the reinvestment or *compounding* of interest back into the account. In the traditional world of finance, this is where the analysis of compound interest stops. If the dentist likes the end projection of $432,194, he will move forward with this investment decision. Unfortunately, however, the dentist just made a financial decision without a complete set of facts. As with every other financial decision, when outputs are created, costs are generated as well, and the decision to compound interest is no different. As such, during the investment period, the dentist will also have paid taxes totaling $99,658 from another pocket for a net result of $332,536. This is the real economic result of compounding interest in this client scenario (see Table 4.3, on the next page).

YEAR	BALANCE B.O.Y. ($)	BALANCE E.O.Y. ($)	INTEREST EARNED ($)	ANNUAL TAX ($)	CUMU-LATIVE TAXES ($)
1	100,000	105,000	5000	1,500	1,500
2	105,000	110,250	5,250	1,575	3,075
3	110,250	115,763	5,513	1,654	4,729
4	115,763	121,551	5,788	1,736	6,465
5	121,551	127,628	6,078	1,823	8,288
6	127,628	134,010	6,381	1,914	10,203
7	134,010	140,710	6,700	2,010	12,213
8	140,710	147,746	7,036	2,111	14,324
9	147,746	155,133	7,387	2,216	16,540
10	155,133	162,889	7,757	2,327	18,867
11	162,889	171,034	8,144	2,443	21,310
12	171,034	179,586	8,522	2,566	23,876
13	179,586	188,565	8,979	2,694	26,569
14	188,565	197,993	9,428	2,828	29,398
15	197,993	207,893	9,900	2,970	32,368
16	207,893	218,287	10,395	3,118	35,486
17	218,287	229,202	10,914	3,274	38,761
18	229,202	240,662	11,460	3,438	42,199
19	240,662	252,695	12,033	3,610	45,809
20	252,695	265,330	12,635	3,790	49,599
21	265,330	278,596	13,266	3,980	53,579
22	278,596	292,526	13,930	4,179	57,758
23	292,526	307,152	14,626	4,388	62,146
24	307,152	322,510	15,358	4,607	66,753
25	322,510	338,635	16,125	4,838	71,591
26	338,635	355,567	16,932	5,080	76,670
27	355,567	373,346	17,778	5,334	82,004
28	373,346	392,013	18,667	5,600	87,604
29	392,013	411,615	19,601	5,880	93,484
30	411,615	432,194	20,581	6,174	99,658

Table 4.3

Tim

Many times, dentists are under the impression that if they want to improve their financial situation, they must first be willing to move their current investments to the newest and best products or investments available today. Now don't get me wrong, this can be the best situation in a limited number of cases due to high costs, unfavorable tax treatment, limited access, and minimum benefits, to name a few. However, in client situations we encounter, it is rarely necessary for a client to liquidate investments to reinvest elsewhere. As we stated earlier in our book, the products we own do not drive financial success. Instead, financial success is driven by the strategies we implement as supported by our products. The best financial decisions are not about *what* to invest in, but, rather, about *how* we position our money in the Financial Treatment Plan.

A question that Mart and I always ask ourselves when preparing a Financial Treatment Plan for a new client is, How do we improve the dentist's financial situation without adding new money or increasing the underlying risk for the dentist? At the same time, we want to find a second use (at a minimum) for each available dollar, which allows us to create additional assets, improve the plan's overall results, and add more benefits. A question to ask yourself is, If this type of planning is possible, why wouldn't I want it?

With these new objectives in mind, let's look at an alternative solution for the compound interest situation we just examined. The original investment of $100,000 remains unchanged. However, the annual interest earned on this account will not be compounded back into the investment. Instead, starting in the second year of the investment, the interest will be pulled out of the account at end of each year and moved into a Roth IRA using a back-door strategy. After year two, the $5,000 interest earned on the after-tax investment will be moved into the Roth IRA where it will earn the same 5 percent interest going forward. At the end of year thirty, the after-tax investment will have its original principal of $100,000 and the Roth IRA will have grown to $332,194. The total gross output for this scenario is the same $432,194 (see Figure 4.3 for a visual overview of this scenario).

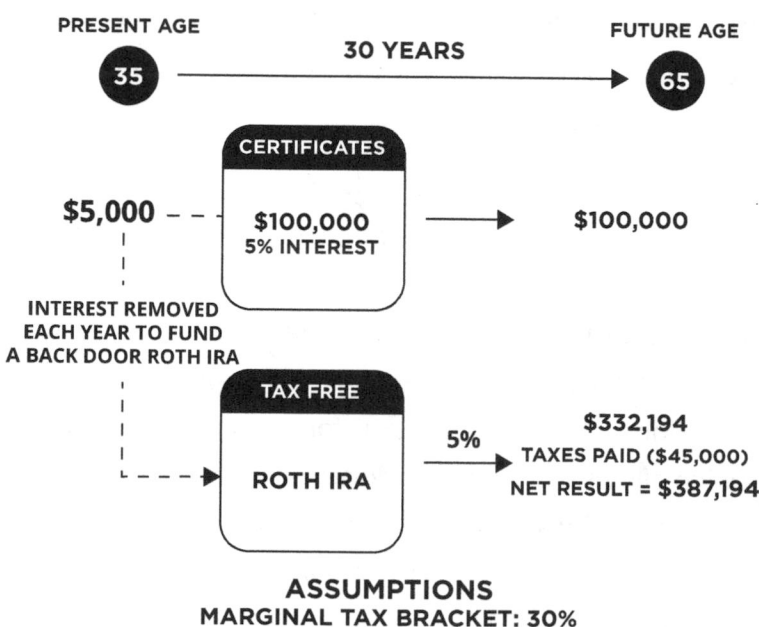

Figure 4.3

As with the original scenario we discussed, the alternative scenario also involved costs in the form of taxes paid in order to produce its gross output. In this case however, the total taxes paid were reduced to $45,000 because the annual taxable interest of $5,000 was removed each year from the taxable account and deposited into the tax-free environment of the Roth IRA. The annual tax in this scenario was flattened at $1,500 ($5,000 x .30) per year, over thirty years for a total of $45,000.

Using the same assets (but in a different way) produced a net result in this scenario of $387,194, versus a net result of $332,536 when interest was simply left to compound in a taxable account. The difference of $54,658 represents a 16 percent improvement as a result of finding an effective second use for the interest-earned dollars in the alternative solution. Can you imagine how the efficiency of your Financial Treatment Plan grows exponentially over time as you find additional uses for each dollar?

A final point to consider when examining these two scenarios is the potential income that can be generated from each result at retirement. Assuming a dentist retires at the end of the thirty-year period under review, how much income can these assets generate assuming an interest-only withdrawal at 5 percent? A detailed breakdown follows on the next page:

	INTEREST COMPOUNDED	ALTERNATIVE SOLUTION
After-tax investments	$432,194	$100,000
Roth IRA	- 0 -	$332,194
Total assets	$432,194	$432,194
INCOME GENERATED @ 5%		
Income from after-tax investments	$21,610	$5,000
Income from Roth IRA (taxable equivalent)*	- 0 -	$23,728
TOTAL INCOME	**$21,610**	**$28,728**

* The taxable equivalent assumes a 30 percent tax bracket.

Table 4.4

The point to take away from this example is that the alternative solution delivered the same gross output of $432,194, as compared to the compound interest scenario. The alternative solution, however, generated $332,194 of tax-free assets. This resulted in a $7,118 or a 33 percent increase in taxable income over the compound interest strategy. All of this was accomplished in the alternative solution without increasing the dentist's investment risk and with the reduced costs of $54,658 in the form of taxes paid. In addition, there were opportunity costs recovered on the tax savings. This is why financial success is not a simple math equation. If your planning is a simple math equation, you will lose the game and take a pay cut in your golden years.

For most, the debunking of these myths goes against everything they've ever been taught about money. But the four myths we've addressed, or debunked here, are just the tip of the iceberg. Making financial decisions based on these myths will cost you hundreds of thousands—and more likely millions—of dollars over a lifetime. Imagine recapturing this lost wealth at no out-of-pocket cost to you and your family! Hundreds of thousands—and possibly millions—more dollars to enjoy in retirement with less risk and the opportunity to be incredibly charitable.

The best way to test any financial decision is to measure it in an evidence-based way. When you have an economic model as the basis for a Financial Treatment Plan, results become very clear. With a Financial Treatment Plan you are able to measure and verify everything. It allows you to see the costs and the benefits of your financial decisions as well as the money gained and lost. More importantly, a Financial Treatment Plan allows an individual to cut through the sales hype and unfounded opinions that are rampant in the traditional financial world and make financial decisions solely based on economic facts. This is the only way to determine if a financial strategy is an economic truth or a myth.

Chapter 5

PUTTING YOUR MONEY IN POSITION

• • •

It's not how much money you make, but how much money you keep, how hard it works for you, and how many generations you keep it for.

—ROBERT KIYOSAKI, AUTHOR OF *RICH DAD, POOR DAD*

Many dentists believe that a successful retirement is dependent solely on how big a retiree's pile of assets *is* upon retirement. Because of this view, most dentists we meet with have maxed out the retirement plans for both themselves and their spouse in order to accumulate those assets. Depending upon the cash flow of a dental practice, a dentist may even adopt a cash balance plan as part of an overall retirement plan. Also, as we've discussed, many dentists have been advised to accelerate their debt repayment, buy term insurance, and compound their interest. As proven in the last chapter, all of these recommendations are problematic for long-term wealth enjoyment.

If these pieces, which are part of many traditional financial plans, were the key to the retirement puzzle, dentists would be retiring earlier not later. The fact is that dentists today are retiring even later than before. A recent report on retirement published by the ADA found the average retirement age of dentists is now 68.8, up two years from just a few years earlier.[16] We find this statistic troubling for many reasons, but primarily because delaying retirement is sad and unnecessary.

The average dentist is now retiring close to age sixty-nine. That tells us that many dentists are needlessly missing out on the best decade of their life. A recent Stanford University study asked eighty-year-old couples, "If they could relive any decade over again, what would it be? " Their answer was overwhelmingly the decade of their sixties for four reasons: 1) their kids were out of the house, 2) they still had money, 3) their health was good, and most significantly, 4) they knew what was important in life!

Later retirement for the average dentist is happening despite the fact that dentists make a good income throughout their career and, typically, save a fair amount of money over their lifetime. This leads us to believe that the traditional way of positioning assets for retirement is seriously flawed.

The reasons that dentists delay retirement are numerous, but the most significant inhibitor to a dentist's long-term financial well-being is that it takes time for dentists to get their feet on the ground. Huge student loan obligations, starting or buying into a practice, purchasing a home, and perhaps starting a family can be significant financial obligations. This is on top of the fact that dentists are not able to start their earnings career until their mid to late twenties at the earliest. By default, the late career start will shorten the number of years available to accumulate wealth.

---

16   "2010 Survey on Retirement and Investment," American Dental Association.

A lack of understanding of the exponential curve of life is another factor that contributes to slow wealth creation and a later retirement date for many. By not knowing the importance of the exponential curve, and its impact on long-term wealth building, dentists set themselves up to lose millions of dollars before and during retirement.

EXPONENTIAL CURVE OF LIFE

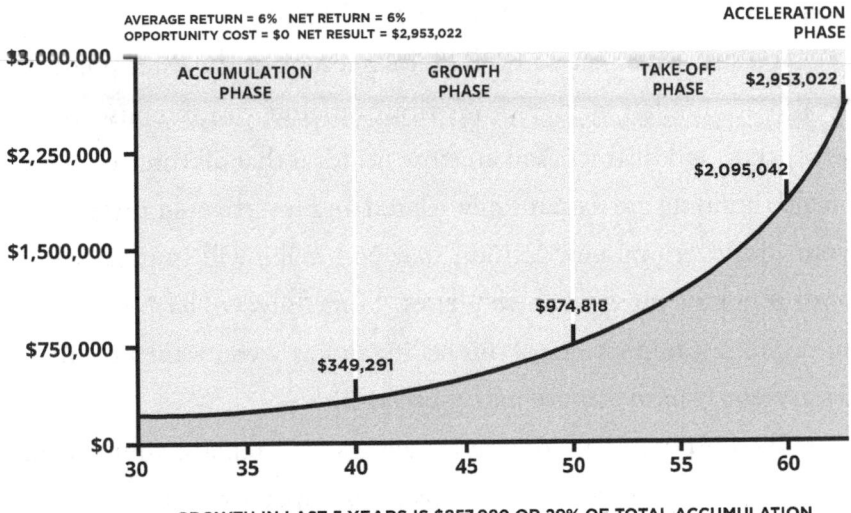

Figure 5.1

Most dentists understand how the exponential curve impacts them in the accumulation phase of their life when they are investing in retirement plans or after-tax investments. The graph above depicts a thirty-five-year time period in which a person is saving $25,000 per year to a retirement plan at an assumed interest rate of 6 percent. New monies contributed to this plan will grow slowly during the accumulation phase or the first ten years of the curve. They pick up steam during the growth phase of the curve (between years eleven and twenty) and take off between the years twenty-one and thirty.

The most significant growth in this example, however ($857,980 or 29 percent of the total accumulation), occurs in the last five years of the curve during the acceleration phase. This graph clearly shows that. Every poor decision made early in a career impacts the end of the curve and, therefore, long-term wealth. The problem for most dentists, however, is that minimal to no consideration is given to the other wealth-building phases—distribution and conservation—and how the exponential curve impacts these. This is where millions of dollars are lost and why retirements are delayed.

It is our hope that you will no longer look at the three phases of wealth accumulation, wealth distribution, and wealth conservation as separate and distinct. You are now mindful that all three phases of wealth building are dynamically related and intertwined throughout your life. Every money decision that you make will impact at least two, if not all three, of these phases. Hopefully, we have impressed upon you the importance of this reality and why you want a Financial Treatment Plan to achieve maximum wealth.

The purpose of all long-term savings is to replace your income in retirement. Regardless of their age, it is imperative that all dentists know and understand the distribution strategy for their retirement accounts and other investments when they first decide to invest. In other words, distribution strategies should be discussed and implemented long before a dentist is ready to retire. In the traditional advisory world, as discussed in the last chapter, dentists are told to maximize their retirement plan contributions at the expense of everything else, with little understanding of how to get the money out thirty years later.

If no distribution strategy is in place at the time of retirement, which is true for most dentists we meet, then by default, a dentist is relegated to accepting an extremely low distribution rate for retirement income. What is a distribution rate? It is the amount of money that can be regularly withdrawn from retirement funds without risking the depletion of those funds during the retiree's lifetime. The simulations that measure these probabilities are called Monte Carlo.

On a side note, we find it funny that the financial industry uses the same verification method to determine the likelihood of not running out of money in retirement as casinos use to measure the probability of winning at the various gambling options they offer. The Monte Carlo simulation both reveals instances that have a high rate of success for the retiree to not run out of money and also shows the scenarios in which a casino will win big through gambling operations. Despite the statistics that are in favor of the casino, we all know people who have won while gambling. At the same time, we also know people who have run out of money in retirement. Our point is simply this: although a Monte Carlo simulation may show a high rate of success, it is not a guaranteed result and may fail. Knowing this, as a retiree, do you really want to base your retirement income on a Monte Carlo safe withdrawal rate? We think not!

As mentioned previously, in the traditional world of finance, where distribution rates are, typically, in the 2–4 percent range, dentists do not have enough time to accumulate the assets that will be required to replace their income in retirement. The solution to this dilemma is to position financial assets over the course of a career in such a way that the distribution rates are in the range of 7 percent (today's rate) to 13 percent (historical high) at retirement. This is a game changer. The retirement income will more than double and increased risk during the accumulation phase will not be incurred.

The proper positioning of assets in your Financial Treatment Plan takes significant pressure off the long-held belief that you need to accumulate a large sum of money in order to replace your income.

For example, dentists would only have to accumulate $3,750,000 in total assets at an 8 percent distribution rate to replace a $300,000 income. In contrast, a safe withdrawal strategy at 3 percent would require dentists to accumulate $10,000,000 by retirement in order to deliver the same income of $300,000. Achieving an increased distribution rate in retirement has very little to do with the investment's rate of return or even the financial product itself. Instead, it has everything to do with the strategy behind the financial products. Wouldn't it be great to not have to depend solely on the rate of return?

It is the marriage of your investments with actuarial science that provides the most income along with guarantees in retirement. What is actuarial science? It is a discipline that assesses financial risks in the finance and insurance fields using mathematical and statistical methods. It applies the mathematics of probability and statistics to define, analyze, and solve the financial implications of uncertain financial events. Life insurance, annuities, and pension plans are the main applications of actuarial science (see Investopedia, s.v. "Actuarial science," https://www.investopedia.com/terms/a/actuarial-science.asp).

The key to an actuarial-based (protected) asset strategy is that to ensure that the amount of the whole life insurance death benefit matches total invested assets at retirement. When this occurs, the only purpose of the retirement assets is to provide an income to the dentist at retirement (see flow diagram, below). This income can be fully maximized and guaranteed with a strategy that provides a 7 percent distribution rate for a sixty-five-year-old male today. The death benefit of life insurance addresses the longevity and estate issues of the wealth conservation phase and allows retirees to fully maximize and enjoy their retirement income today without the fear of running out of money.

Income is fully maximized in retirement when there is a 1:1 ratio of retirement assets to whole life death benefit. The presence of whole life insurance in the Financial Treatment Plan acts as the permission slip for dentists to take the maximum income from their retirement assets. If the money is positioned correctly over the course of time, there should be no additional out-of-pocket cost in order to double the income in retirement. In other words, lifestyle does not need to be changed to implement these strategies. The details of how one implements a protected asset strategy are discussed further in chapters 6 & 7.

Achieving these results is having a game board that provides an evidence-based way of determining where every dollar that comes into our lives should be positioned. The only way to do this is to have a Financial Treatment Plan. Let's take a look at how a Financial Treatment Plan is built from start to finish

A successful Financial Treatment Plan starts with having a solid foundation in place. If this foundation is ignored, or not complete, your financial house can and will crumble at the first occurrence of an unexpected event.

The three cornerstones that make up the foundation of a successful Financial Treatment Plan are maximum protection, a disciplined savings rate of 15 percent at minimum, and a cash liquidity position equal to at least 50 percent of one year's gross household income. We believe that if dentists achieved only these three objectives, they would be light-years ahead of the majority of their peers. Unfortunately, we have yet to meet any dentists who already have these three cornerstones in place when they become our clients. Obviously, a fully implemented Financial Treatment Plan is ideal, but if the foundation of the three cornerstones is missing, the treatment plan will fail at some point. Let's examine the three cornerstones.

The acquisition of maximum insurance coverage is the first cornerstone in the Financial Treatment Plan. Types of insurance coverage included in the treatment plan are: auto, homeowners, liability, disability, health, and life. Some may wonder what maximum insurance coverage represents. The answer is simple. Maximum insurance coverage is nothing more than owning the amount of insurance coverage you would want if the event you insured against were to occur.

As an example, if you were to injure someone in a car accident, how much liability coverage would you want to own? Also, if you became permanently disabled, how much disability income coverage would you want? If you were faced with a major health issue, would you want to own minimum or maximum health insurance coverage? Finally, in the event of your death, how much life insurance would you want to own in order to replace your income for your loved ones?

The amount of coverage desired is different for everyone, depending on the individual's situation. Most dentists would agree, however, that they would want to own the maximum amount of insurance coverage possible if they were to face any of these adverse situations. So shouldn't individuals own maximum insurance coverage today even though they don't know when such a situation is going to occur? The answer to this question is a resounding yes! Why is it, then, that most dentists don't already have the maximum possible insurance coverage? For most dentists, it all comes down to the perceived cost of acquiring insurance coverage. If cost were not an issue, however, would there be any reason not to own maximum protection at all times?

Ideally, these types of coverage can be acquired with little to no out-of-pocket expense to the dentist. Despite what the traditional world of finance will tell you, the cost savings in this area will result more from how these protection assets are purchased than the actual cost of the products themselves. Examination of the dentist's entire Financial Treatment Plan will allow for cost minimization strategies to be implemented in the acquisition of the protection assets.

A comment we hear often is, "I don't want to be overinsured." The fear of being overinsured is not realistic, however, as no insurance company would ever allow this to happen. An insurance company will only replace a specified loss of value and not a penny more. This is the purpose of the underwriting process for all insurance products.

The second cornerstone in the Financial Treatment Plan is establishing a disciplined savings rate of no less than 15 percent of one year's gross household income. If you have a gross income of $300,000, then we want to see $45,000 being saved in the Financial Treatment Plan. This is the target we strive for. The sooner you can get to that point, the better off you will be.

The 15 percent annual savings rate is a minimum target and is needed to offset the wealth-eroding factors of life that we all encounter and that include such things as inflation, taxes, planned obsolescence, technological change, and standard of living increases, to name a few. If a 15 percent savings rate is not obtained, then the dentist is actually going backward from an overall financial stand-point, due to these and other wealth-eroding factors. The discipline of saving is key to a Financial Treatment Plan's success.

The final cornerstone in the foundation of the Financial Treatment Plan and the third step to building a solid financial foundation is to establish strong liquid cash reserves. These reserves should be established even before starting to save funds in a retirement plan. Therefore, the initial goal with our savings is to establish a strong liquidity position. We like to see dentists maintain 50 percent of one year's gross household income in liquid funds. If you are making an annual salary of $300,000, then you want to have $150,000 in liquidity, or six months of your annual gross income. Liquidity can be held in checking, savings, CDs, or money market accounts, and it even includes the cash value of your whole life insurance.

Why do you need so much liquidity? The answer is that if you don't have liquidity, you don't have permission to do anything else in your Financial Treatment Plan. Liquidity is key! Liquidity covers unexpected emergencies and is available for possible investment and business opportunities.

• • • • • • • • • • • • • • • • • • • •

Tim

Years ago, a mentor of mine shared with me his belief that people all have one or two real opportunities fall in their lap at some point during their lifetime. Unfortunately, a high percentage of people never act on these opportunities. He concluded that the reason people don't take action is because they did not have the cash on hand to do so.

For those of you who may believe that maintaining a high cash reserve is inefficient, due to the low interest rate earned on savings today, you are missing the point. I believe that some of the highest rates of return are earned when a 0 percent rate of return meets opportunity. When you have cash on hand, you can react quickly. If you don't have cash on hand, you may miss the opportunity!

• • • • • • • • • • • • • • • • • • • •

The most important reason to maintain some liquidity, however, is to provide peace of mind. Life is a lot different when you have a strong liquidity position in place and the market goes down 30 percent. In this case, if you have cash on hand, you are not as panicked. You may even choose to make an additional investment when the market is down and stock prices are low. This is what successful investors attempt to do. On the other hand, if you only have $5,000 sitting in your bank account and the market goes down 30 percent, you are more likely to panic and make an emotionally charged decision to liquidate your investment account.

Keep in mind that if your liquidity is used for any reason, then it needs to be replenished to reestablish that peace of mind and give you the ability to respond quickly to emergencies and opportunities as they arise. Typically, it will take a dentist several years to establish a liquidity position equal to 50 percent of annual earnings, so do not think it has to be done overnight.

Once liquidity is established, the foundation of the Financial Treatment Plan is set. The foundation of maximum protection, disciplined savings, and solid liquidity protects a dentist against unexpected events and wealth-eroding factors that can destroy a Financial Treatment Plan if left unchecked. This gives dentists total peace of mind as they begin building their long-term future wealth.

In sports, it is often stated that "defense wins championships." We believe that the same holds true when building wealth successfully. The three cornerstones that make up the foundation of the Financial Treatment Plan are the defense of a successful treatment plan. Just as in sports, a Financial Treatment Plan with a highly productive offense will struggle and frequently lose if there are holes in the defense. In order for dentists to achieve maximum wealth, their Financial Treatment Plan needs both a solid defense and offense. Let's examine the rules that comprise a successful offense in a Financial Treatment Plan.

First, compounding interest in after-tax accounts should be avoided. The key takeaway here is that any time you simply put compound interest, dividends, or capital gains back into the same account, you are, in essence, forfeiting your right to use those dollars a second or third time in your Financial Treatment Plan. This results in reduced wealth and benefits. (Please refer back to chapter 4 where the money myth of compound interest was debunked.)

This is where the wealth freedom account (WFA) comes into play. The WFA is a separate checking or savings account whose sole purpose is to capture earnings from plan assets (e.g., interest, dividends, capital gains) or new monies that are being saved in the Financial Treatment Plan. To prevent these monies from being spent in your everyday life, this account is not comingled with your household checking or savings accounts. Instead, the WFA's purpose is to accumulate these excess dollars so that they may be moved elsewhere within the Financial Treatment Plan on a monthly, quarterly, semiannual, or annual basis. Money is moved out of this account to be used in new ways where additional rates of return and benefits are created. This generates exponential growth on your money.

It is at this point that retirement plans first come into existence as part of the Financial Treatment Plan. As stated earlier, it is not the first place your money should go. Nor should you direct 100 percent of your annual savings into a retirement plan. Instead, our rule for savings directed into retirement accounts states that an individual should contribute up to the level of the employer's match. In no case, however, should you contribute more than half of your annual savings rate. As an example, if you are saving at the minimum target rate of 15 percent, you should put no more than 7 percent into a retirement plan. This allows you to build a broadly diversified Financial Treatment Plan that includes retirement assets and other outside investments.

Another point to keep in mind is that all retirement accounts are considered part of the savings component in the Financial Treatment Plan. The savings component is where our safe money resides. As such, we should not take undue risks with these funds. They should be invested in a moderately conservative fashion to help ensure that the plan assets will be there when you are ready to retire. Retirement assets that experience a market correction can decimate plans for retirement.

Is the employer 401(k) match a good thing? Accountants love to tout the benefits of a retirement plan's employer match. Also, the media tells us all the time that an employer match is free money, but is it, really? Maybe yes, maybe no. If you are the owner of the practice and therefore the 401(k) sponsor, the employer match is not a big deal because you are the employer. What this means is that you are matching your own money, so it is not free money, as we are told. When you are an associate or work for a corporation, such as a dental service organization (DSO), the employer match on the plan is a bona fide match because the money is coming from the corporation, not you.

Once the retirement plan is established, any excess funds saved can be directed to the growth component or investment section of the Financial Treatment Plan. This is where your risk money goes, which includes financial assets such as bonds, stocks, and hard assets including collectibles, antiques, artwork, cryptocurrencies, real estate, and business ownership.

The ideal objective in the growth component is to diversify holdings that are invested in the core assets of this component. A heavy concentration in any one of the core assets, whether it is bonds, stocks, or hard assets, will place undue risk on your overall Financial Treatment Plan. Outside influences, such as declining interest rates, stock market corrections, a soft rental or real estate market, or unexpected challenges in your own dental practice, can absolutely devastate a Financial Treatment Plan if you are heavily concentrated in only one core asset of the growth component. You want to strive for balance and diversification among all these assets.

Again, any dividends, interest, capital gains, rental earnings from real estate, and excess income from businesses are captured and moved back through your WFA. As discussed earlier, when monies accumulate in your WFA, you will consider utilizing those funds in one of three ways: 1) to pay down debt, 2) to enhance your insurance coverage, or 3) to make additional investments elsewhere. Your decision will be thought out and intentional, rather than an automatic reinvestment of the dividend, interest, or capital gain that creates an increasing compounding tax over time (read chapter 4 on the compound interest myth). As money is moved elsewhere within your Financial Treatment Plan, the velocity, or money multiplier effect, will come into play as you get a second, third, and fourth use of your dollars over time. This is how the rainmakers make their money, so why shouldn't you do it that way as well?

Proper positioning and placement of each financial asset is essential for building wealth in the most efficient and effective manner. In addition, eliminating unnecessary costs and risks in your Financial Treatment Plan will add hundreds of thousands if not millions of dollars of additional wealth to your balance sheet over your lifetime. However, as stated several times previously in this book, the accumulation of numerous assets by retirement is meaningless if you don't have exit or distribution strategies in place that will turn those assets into an income stream. A seven-figure net worth means nothing if you don't have the ability to spend and enjoy those funds during your retirement without the fear of running out of money.

Your wealth potential is maximized when you fully embrace the underlying rules of the Financial Treatment Plan described in this book. If you choose to ignore any step in the process of the Financial Treatment Plan, or implement the steps out of order, you will not achieve the maximum results. More importantly, you will have limited use and enjoyment of your money over a lifetime.

Another key principle to embrace when building wealth is keeping your money in motion. In other words, every time you find an additional use for a dollar, you will pick up another rate of return and additional benefits that further enhance your wealth. Money that is moving through your Financial Treatment Plan is like blood in your body. When blood is not moving, it can clot and cause death. When money sits in one place for too long it gets stale and eventually rots due to the numerous wealth-eroding factors discussed previously. Stale or inactive money is the financial cancer that can decimate personal finances. The incorporation of a wealth freedom account within a Financial Treatment Plan is the key to curing this financial cancer. Monies flow continuously into this account and are then redirected to other parts of the Financial Treatment Plan, much as the heart pumps blood to different parts of the body.

Implementing these evidence-based rules takes a lot of pressure off your accumulated assets. Because the assets in the Financial Treatment Plan are balanced with actuarial science, you no longer have to chase an elusive rate of return in the hopes of building a huge pile of assets. The strategic, combined positioning of the assets in the Financial Treatment Plan is more important than the individual assets themselves. Ideally, these rules, along with keeping your money in motion, are essential to positioning your money for full income replacement with guarantees in retirement. This process also affords you the opportunity to retire sooner rather than later. The only way to do this is to have a Financial Treatment Plan to guide you down the financial path toward ultimate enjoyment of your money both today and in the future.

Chapter 6

LANDING YOUR MONEY SAFELY

● ● ●

Know what you own and why you own it.

—PETER LYNCH

According to an old adage, you should not spend your principal in retirement because you will need it to generate interest for the rest of your life. That adage simply does not hold water any more. It only works if you want to take a pay cut in retirement. Less income is obviously not the objective for anyone.

When we ask dentists how they expect to spend their money in retirement, most of them answer, "We are just going to live off the interest of what we have accumulated and we will be fine." In truth, they have not given any deep thought to what that statement actually means. According to a New York Life survey, 77 percent of respondents reported that they did not know how much they could withdraw annually in retirement without running the risk of outliving their assets.[17] The fact of the matter is that in the world we live in today, *nobody* can live off the interest generated by assets

---

17 "77% of Americans Don't Understand How to Safely Withdraw from Their Nest Eggs in Retirement," New York Life, April 26, 2016, https://www.newyorklife.com/newsroom/2016/withdraw-from-nest-eggs-in-retirement.

if income replacement is the goal. Whether it is saving accounts, laddered CDs, bonds, dividends, or any other investment, right now the interest earned by that principal would range from 1 percent to 4 percent. Honestly, will that interest allow you to have the retirement you want?

Let's assume you have accumulated $3,000,000 at retirement and use a 3 percent safe withdrawal rate for your retirement income. In this scenario, the investment will generate $90,000 of income each year. If you managed to accumulate that much money, in all likelihood, you were probably earning $250,000 to $300,000 a year as a dentist. If you planned on living off the income generated by interest in retirement, then the $90,000 of investment income in this example does not go very far in replacing your preretirement income. In fact, if you were looking to fully replace your income of $250,000 in retirement, you would have to accumulate roughly $8.3 million in assets. For many, accumulating this sum of money would be impossible due to either a lack of time or the inability to set aside this amount of savings.

The old adage of living off your interest in retirement may sound like a great idea, but in reality, this strategy will only set you up to lead a retired life of quiet economic desperation.

In the traditional financial world, where retirees' piles of assets are solely concentrated in their retirement plan, they will unknowingly have placed a lot of pressure on these assets to perform during the golden years and provide an income for as long as the retirees live. For a married couple, this income needs to provide for two lifetimes, which can each be as long as thirty-five years, or more in some situations. Running out of money is one of the greatest fears for a retiree.[18]

---

18   Ryan Derousseau, "4 Financial Fears About Retirement, And How to Overcome Them," *U.S. News & World Report*, January, 20, 2017, https://money.usnews.

No one should allow this to happen. If a retiree wants to leave a legacy to anyone, it will need to come from these assets. As a result, retirees are left trying to preserve capital for longevity or estate purposes at the expense of accepting an increased distribution rate for income during retirement. This situation is further complicated by the fact that a Monte Carlo distribution rate of 3 percent does not guarantee an income stream for life, as the assets will be spent over time. We believe this is unacceptable.

Upon retirement, many begin to realize that there is a lot of pressure on the pile of assets concentrated in their retirement plans. They also realize that they have no control over how this money will grow or diminish, because it is subject to market fluctuations, interest rates, and tax law changes. All of a sudden, they are living in a world of fear because they realize that they have minimal control over their assets. They remember the old adage and think, *Okay, we'll try to live off our interest.* Then, they quickly realize they can't do that either. Their next thought is, *I need to be in the market. My advisor tells me that the market has historically delivered over a 10 percent rate of return.* On average, this is true, but when was the last time you received the same rate of return year after year? Never! Market returns are variable. You may get a positive return one year and a negative return the next year, and so on. Remember 2008? This is a significant dilemma, as rates of return will fluctuate from year to year. During retirement, this volatility can have a dramatic impact on your golden years.

The accepted retirement option in traditional retirement planning is to take money at what is referred to as a safe withdrawal rate (Monte Carlo distribution), as discussed in the last chapter, from retirement assets. Years ago, these safe withdrawal rates were upward

---

com/investing/articles/2017-01-20/4-financial-fears-about-retirement-and-how-to-overcome-them.

of 7 percent. Even the legendary investor Peter Lynch said that a 7 percent withdrawal rate was an appropriate distribution rate for an all-stock portfolio.[19] Over time, a 7 percent withdrawal rate has proven to be way too high as markets go up and down unpredictably. Amazingly, 58 percent of people surveyed in 2016 still felt that a safe withdrawal rate in excess of 4 percent was acceptable, with 31 percent believing over 10 percent was safe.[20]

In today's world, the accepted safe withdrawal rate is between 3 and 4 percent. Without proper planning, dentists will fall into this trap at retirement. Unfortunately, due to volatile markets, low interest rates, and unexpected life changes, even at a low 3–4 percent withdrawal rate, there is still a chance that dentists and their spouse could run out of money if they live long enough.

Many of our dental clients are hoping to retire as early as age sixty. That means their money may have to last them for thirty-five years or longer in retirement, which could be longer than their entire working career. Consider this statistic: a 3 percent safe withdrawal over thirty years in retirement has successfully funded individuals and kept them from running out of money 97 percent of the time throughout the history of the market. If you live five years longer, for a total of thirty-five years, your chances of not running out of money during retirement now drops to 91 percent at that same 3 percent safe withdrawal rate. That means there is almost a one in ten chance that you will run out of money over a thirty-five-year time frame when using a 3 percent annual withdrawal rate. These numbers are obviously more ominous with a 4 percent annual distribution.

---

19   Peter Lynch, "From the Archives: Fear of Crashing," *Worth, March 9, 2017,* *https://www.worth.com/from-the-archives-fear-of-crashing.*

20   "77% of Americans Don't Understand How to Safely Withdraw from Their Nest Eggs in Retirement," New York Life.

Many of you may think that running out of money in retirement will never happen to you. After all, that's the kind of thing that happens to other people. Our question is—what if it *is* you? What do you do then? What is your back-up plan? What if you retire and the very next year there is a drop in the market, as there was in 2008, and you lose 40 percent of your investments? Does that change your retirement? The answer is a definite yes. Remember our wrapper discussion in chapter 2 and the objective to create plans that work under all circumstances. Failure cannot be an option!

• • • • • • • • • • • • • • • • • • •

Mart

I was at a conference where Steve Forbes was speaking. He said something along the lines of, "With all of the technological advancements in healthcare these days, the average lifespan will increase by ten to fifteen years."

Therefore, we may live much longer than we can even envision today. As a result, our greatest risk in retirement will be outliving our assets. We can't know how long we will live. This means that our retirement money may have to last a very long period of time. Therefore, having more guaranteed income, and not just a pile of assets, is key to a successful retirement.

• • • • • • • • • • • • • • • • • • •

Again, when we talk about the probabilities of running out of money, people always feel it will never happen to them. They believe they have smarter advisors on their team, or that they have the ability to see things coming. For a proper perspective on this, let's take finances off the table and consider another situation. Let's assume that you and your significant other arrive at the airport to leave for an extended weekend getaway. Before you board the plane, however, the pilot comes across the intercom and says, "I just checked the weather and we are going to have a fantastic flight, with the exception of a fifteen-minute period when we will be flying through some really dangerous storms. Don't worry though! I have done my calculations and there is a 90 percent chance that we will land safely on the other end." This means, of course, that there is a 10 percent chance that the plane will crash.

Knowing this, how many of you are willing to still get on that plane? Even with only a 10 percent chance of the plane crashing, when we ask a seminar audience this question, no one raises a hand to say yes. People would rather head to the rental car desk to rent a car or wait for the next flight.

Retirement can also be a life-and-death situation. If you wouldn't board a plane that has a 10 percent chance of crashing and ending your life, why would you take a 10 percent chance of running out of money during your retirement? Running out of money in retirement may not result in your death, but it most certainly leads to a living death.

It's interesting that people will accept the chance of running out of money in retirement, as if they have no other options. When getting on a plane, you want 100 percent certainty that the plane will land safely. Why wouldn't you want 100 percent certainty when it comes to your income in retirement as well? The reason may be that while the plane crash has a definite result (you know if that plane goes down, it is very unlikely you will survive), you may think that if you run out of money there will be a back-up plan.

You think, *Well, maybe the kids will step in, or maybe I can go back to work.* If you are running out of money toward the end of your retirement, however, it often means you are seventy-five or eighty years old. How employable will you be at that age? Will your skills still be up to par? How likely is it that you will be hired? Would you really want to ask your children to support you?

The biggest issue with a safe withdrawal rate of 3 percent, even if it were guaranteed to continue providing for the duration of your retirement, is the low income it yields in retirement. You are, essentially, saying, "Okay, I am going to make it, but I am not going to live life to its fullest." We think that is unacceptable. Why not have 100 percent income replacement *and* live life to the fullest? In the traditional financial world, you may make it 90 percent of the time, but you will be taking less income. Great, you made it, but you did not live the life you expected in retirement!

● ● ● ● ● ● ● ● ● ● ● ● ● ● ● ● ●

Tim

As an example, let's use a 3 percent withdrawal rate on $1,000,000 for the decade of the 1990s. At the end of those ten years, which hosted the greatest bull market in the history of the stock market, your million dollars would have grown to about $4,300,000 after withdrawing $30,000 annually for your retirement income. Life would have been great, and you probably would have been thinking that you could adjust and take more income annually.

The very next decade, however, from 2000 to the end of 2009—the so-called lost decade of the stock market—if you had withdrawn the same amount of $30,000 each year, you would only have had $593,000 in your retirement account balance at the end of ten years. This is an unbelievable but real difference, based on the sequence of market returns dilemma.

Now, let's look at the most recent decade, from 2008 to 2017. At the end of 2017, assuming the same annual withdrawal of $30,000, your account balance would total a little over $1.6 million. Most people would be happy with this result over a ten-year period. The problem is, at the end of 2008, or the first year of retirement in this example, the retiree's account balance would only have been $611,000 due to the stock market crash of 2008. Our bet is that people who were down almost 40 percent in their retirement account after the first year would not have stayed in this retirement strategy long enough to see the $1.6 million at the end of ten years. During the stock market crash, most retirees would have bailed out of their investments and done something different with their money. It then becomes an emergency, as you have less money and are staring at a reduced retirement income in the face. As a result, you are going to have to make some difficult decisions, such as downsizing your home, selling a second home, traveling less, dropping your country club membership, and making other cuts in your budget or lifestyle.

• • • • • • • • • • • • • • • • • • • •

Many dentists have very limited time to spend on financial planning. They are busy with their practice and life gets in the way.

Due to business, family, and other outside commitments, they have no time to meet with their team of advisors. Their practices are thriving, their children are growing up too fast, and all of a sudden, they are sixty years old and they have done very little to truly prepare for retirement. They find themselves in this position not because they have failed to take advice, but rather, the advice they did take came from the traditional retirement planning world where accepting a 50 percent pay cut in retirement is commonplace.

Up to this point, dentists have made and spent a lot of money and lived a great life but oftentimes were not diligent savers or saved money in the wrong places. Maybe they had a retirement plan, a practice to sell, possibly some real estate in the form of an office building, or a cash balance plan, in addition to other investments, but they have done no strategic positioning of their assets.

What's the answer to this? First, dentists have to understand that traditional retirement planning has significant problems. If they don't understand the problems created by their traditional retirement plans, they will never accept a solution for the problems. Our initial step is to help dentists better understand where they are financially today. We show them what they can expect if they continue on their current paths, based on the assets they have accrued at this moment. We also look at present contributions and any possible new money that dentists anticipate saving, going forward. Based on an assumed rate of return, and the number of years dentists have before retirement, they will now be able to visualize their current retirement path. We then allow them to discover that without an exit strategy in retirement, they will be looking at an income in retirement equivalent to a 3 percent withdrawal rate on their investments, and worse yet, accepting a retirement income that is not guaranteed. When this stark reality sinks in, dentists realize this is not the retirement path they want.

Once there is agreement that they do not want to stay on their current retirement path, the next step is to look at how they can solve their retirement dilemma using the same inputs and assets they have today. We are not talking about taking additional money from their pockets. We are instead helping them discover more efficient ways to use the same inputs in a Financial Treatment Plan that will create more long-term wealth and benefits with no additional out-of-pocket costs or increased risk.

These inputs can include money going into their savings accounts, retirement plans, or different investment accounts. Other inputs may include overpayments made on student loans or prepayments on their mortgage and other debts. We also look at the internal efficiency of assets already accumulated to date. For example, are interest, dividends, and capital gains being automatically reinvested in an after-tax account? It is our job to help individuals discover more efficient ways to use the assets and resources that are part of their financial lives.

In doing so, however, it is not appropriate for us, or anyone else for that matter, to simply say, "This is what you should do with your money" without first providing verification. You work hard for your money and financial decisions are too important to base them on opinion only. As such, you should demand verification from your advisors prior to making any financial decision. This is where our Financial Treatment Plan comes into play.

We start by analyzing the present money decisions made by a dentist. It is important to understand all of the positive results related to these decisions as well as any negative results that may exist. After all, if the net result of a financial decision were neutral or negative to your overall wealth building, wouldn't you want to know about that? Of course you would!

Once our dental clients are aware of their present situation, we introduce alternative strategies (using the same resources) and compare them side-by-side with the clients' present strategy. Using the Financial Treatment Plan, the positive and negatives results of each decision can be economically verified. As such, sales hype, opinion, and emotion are removed from the analysis. This allows dentists to make a financial decision based on economics and nothing else.

Through the use of the Financial Treatment Plan, our dental clients will discover the economic results generated from the placement of each dollar. Our goal is to create an exit strategy that will help our dental clients more than double their income in retirement. At the same time, we want to eliminate any possibility of our clients having to accept a safe withdrawal rate of only 3 percent at age sixty-five, with no guarantees. Instead, we want individuals to experience 7–8 percent (or higher) distribution rates from their assets at retirement, *with* guarantees.

How do we do that? Part of the answer lies in the incorporation of actuarial science as part of the Financial Treatment Plan. This was first mentioned in the last chapter and requires that whole life insurance and/or distribution specific annuities are part of the overall plan in some capacity. Ideally, we want to achieve a 1:1 ratio of the total whole life insurance death benefit to the total value of outside investments and retirement plans. If one area is more heavily weighted than the other, we will not achieve maximum results. In other words, it is bad to have excessive assets without life insurance, or to have too much life insurance without the assets. Balance is the key. These things are essential to fully replace preretirement income throughout retirement.

● ● ● ● ● ● ● ● ● ● ● ● ● ● ● ● ● ● ●

Tim

Too often what keeps dentists from adding whole life insurance to their financial plan is a perception that it's too expensive or that the advisor is going to receive a big commission to their detriment. As are the many myths we have discussed, these beliefs are misinformation promoted by traditional advisors, accountants, and financial gurus. As an example, in Plan A, a dentist is contributing $50,000 to his retirement plan and investments. In Plan B, a dentist is contributing $50,000 that is allocated between a retirement plan, investments, and whole life insurance. Is there any difference in the total annual savings entering plan A or Plan B? The answer is no. What is expensive is not having all three asset types in the Financial Treatment Plan at the time of retirement.

● ● ● ● ● ● ● ● ● ● ● ● ● ● ● ● ● ● ●

To achieve multiple streams of income in retirement, it is absolutely necessary that during their working years, dentists allocate their annual savings equally to their retirement plan, outside investments, and whole life insurance. Let's examine some of the possible income streams that are available after retirement.

The most obvious income stream that every dentist receives at retirement (assuming the program remains viable) is Social Security. We believe this to be true for dentists who are within ten years of retirement today. Unfortunately, for dentists starting their careers today, Social Security will likely be different by the time they retire.

Other income stream possibilities include interest or dividends from investments, income streams from annuities, spend-down strategies on assets, and maximum versus minimum distributions from a retirement plan. Rental income from an office building or other properties can also be a great income stream during retirement. Additionally, you could have a charitable trust that produces income (more on this later). There might also be collectibles, cryptocurrencies, and master limited partnerships. Almost anything that produces income can be an income source. In reality, you could have ten or more different sources or streams of income in retirement. When this happens, you are positioned to receive an income that resembles roaring rapids rather than a trickle.

Most working dentists that we encounter are on the path of only receiving a trickle of income in retirement. This is because they will have only three to four sources of retirement income. These typically include Social Security, a retirement plan, and proceeds from a dental practice sale. If dentists happened to own the building they practiced in, they may add a rental income in retirement. To fully replace the dentist's income, however, there should be many more streams of income!

One question we are often asked is, if you are taking the same dollars and allocating them in different places within the Financial Treatment Plan, how do you not end up with just the same money in the end?

If you had a choice of accumulating either $1,676,000 (Dentist A) or $1,267,000 (Dentist B) of assets at retirement, which dentist would you choose to be? The obvious choice here is Dentist A with $1,676,000 in assets. I mean, who would not want an additional $409,000 of assets in retirement? For most, having the biggest pile of assets at retirement is the goal they have been advised to chase.

Using the same set of facts, you are now informed that Dentist

A can only derive an income of $50,000 a year from accumulated assets after retirement. This is due to the fact that no exit or distribution strategy is built into Dentist A's plan and by default, she is forced to accept a 3 percent safe withdrawal from her assets in retirement. Not only does this method provide minimum income to the retiree, but the income is not guaranteed, meaning it is subject to market and interest rate fluctuations throughout the dentist's retirement years. As a result, Dentist A is not able to fully enjoy her retirement assets.

On the other hand, Dentist B did build a retirement distribution strategy into his Financial Treatment Plan using actuarial science, so at retirement he could receive $67,000 a year in income from his total assets of $1,267,000. In addition, the annual income for Dentist B is 100 percent guaranteed. Knowing this additional information, which dentist would you choose to be now, Dentist A or Dentist B?

Without exception, with this new information, individuals will unanimously choose to be Dentist B in retirement, as they want more income to spend and enjoy. Having more assets in retirement means nothing if it does not equate to more retirement income. There are only two types of income in retirement: one that is guaranteed and one that is not guaranteed. Most retirees prefer guaranteed income if given a choice. Guarantees provide peace of mind and eliminate the uncertainty and related stress induced by market corrections and interest rate fluctuations that can and will occur during a dentist's retirement years.

Some may ask, how is the scenario described above even possible? After all, Dentist B has $409,000 less in assets at retirement, but more income to spend and enjoy. As we said earlier in this book, you should always demand verification of financial alternatives. With that in mind, let's verify each of these financial alternatives for Dentist A and Dentist B.

In our example, both dentists are thirty-five years old, and we are examining a thirty-year time frame until they reach age sixty-five. The dentists' assumed tax bracket is 30 percent and their investment rate of return is 6 percent. In this scenario, each dentist is saving the equivalent of $20,000, pretax, each year. They have identical situations but choose different financial paths.

Dentist A is simply saving her $20,000 each year into her retirement plan. Over a thirty-year period at a 6 percent rate of return, Dentist A's retirement account will grow to $1,676,000 by age sixty-five. Again, this is a large sum of money, but keep in mind that this money is essentially inaccessible until retirement.

Dentist B, on the other hand, takes those same dollars but only directs $11,500 to his retirement plan each year. At age sixty-five, assuming the same 6 percent rate of return, Dentist B has accumulated $964,000 in his retirement plan. The remaining $8,500 of pretax money, or in this case $5,950 of after-tax money (assuming a 30 percent tax bracket) was directed to the purchase of a whole life policy on Dentist B that has an initial death benefit of $472,000. At age sixty-five, the whole life death benefit on Dentist B will have grown to $668,000 and its cash value will be $304,000. Thus, at age sixty-five, Dentist B will have amassed total cash assets of $1,267,000 and have a whole life death benefit of $668,000.

At sixty-five, Dentist A will have a retirement plan with $1,676,000 and nothing else. Dentist A has no exit or distribution strategy built into her plan and by default she will accept some form of a safe withdrawal rate (Monte Carlo distribution) from her retirement plan assets. Today, that accepted withdrawal rate is 3 percent, or in this example, $50,000 of retirement income each year.

• • • • • • • • • • • • • • • • • •

Tim

When retirement assets by themselves are the sole income source, a lot of pressure is placed on them due to three factors:

1. The retirement assets have to provide an income stream throughout the retirement years. Desire for income in retirement does not go away because the market happens to experience a 20 percent market correction. It can be devastating to a retiree when the market takes a hit like this and the retiree still needs income to survive.

2. The retirement assets need to last a lifetime. In other words, retirees will be in trouble if the assets are exhausted before their death. If they are married, then these assets must support two lifetimes and not just one. Depending on their age at the start of their retirement, they could be dependent on these assets as long as thirty-five years, or longer. Remember—retirement can last longer than a career.

3. A legacy (e.g., left to a spouse, children, or charities) must also come from these assets, which may cause the retiree to preserve principal at the expense of taking an adequate income in retirement.

If not addressed properly and eliminated in retirement, these three factors will add undue stress. As we have said, due to one or more of these retirement pressures, most retirees are leading quiet lives of economic desperation, which will be your retirement world, too, if the bulk of your retirement income is derived at a safe withdrawal rate.

• • • • • • • • • • • • • • • • • • •

Dentist B, however, is in a much different situation at retirement. This is due to the fact that he owns a guaranteed whole life death benefit of $668,000 (tax-free) at age sixty-five. This tax-free death benefit will pass on to a spouse, children, or charities at the time of his death. In essence, the tax-free death benefit takes care of any legacy considerations that Dentist B may have. As a result, all the retirement plan assets have to do is provide an income stream to the dentist and his spouse that will last over their respective lifetimes.

In this example, this was achieved on a guaranteed basis by trading the retirement plan assets of $964,000 at age sixty-five for a single premium immediate annuity (SPIA) with a single life option on the dentist only. In today's interest rate environment, this will provide an annual guaranteed income stream of $67,000 ($964,000 x .07). This income is paid as long as the dentist is alive. Upon the death of the dentist, the life insurance death benefit will be paid out to the named beneficiaries (e.g., spouse, children, or charities) to replace the assets that were spent in retirement. The strategy described here is what we refer to as a protected asset strategy.

Now, when we look at the two retirement income options for Dentist A of $50,000 per year and Dentist B of $67,000 per year, which one would you want? Both results for Dentist A and Dentist B were achieved with the same annual inputs, yet Dentist B realized a $17,000, or 34 percent, increase in income at retirement. Also, Dentist B's income is 100 percent guaranteed and not subject to market risk. The icing on the cake for Dentist B is that the dividends on his whole life policy can be used as another income stream if necessary. Unfortunately, Dentist A cannot say the same for her retirement income. Most dentists clearly want to be Dentist B, who has more retirement income—income that is guaranteed—and enjoys the certainty that any legacy concerns have been addressed.

Please keep in mind that the solution shared in this example is one of many possible alternatives and is dependent upon individuals' personal situations as well as their wants and desires. In other words, there is no one-size-fits-all solution when it comes to retirement planning. The key is having flexibility and more options to choose from.

A big fallacy in the investment world is that in order to achieve a high rate of return, you have to take more risk. This may be true in the microeconomic world, but not in the macroeconomic world. Why not have more money and more income with less risk? (That is one of our wealth objectives discussed in chapter 2.) The above example proves that premise very clearly because it considers the big picture. In other words, you can have more income in retirement without chasing a high rate of return and assuming more risk when efficient distribution strategies are built in to the Financial Treatment Plan.

One last thing: when assets are macroeconomically positioned in a Financial Treatment Plan, the total assets accumulated will be virtually the same as those accumulated under a traditional plan. This means that, as Dentist B, you can have your cake and eat it, too, by having the $1,676,000 of assets that Dentist A has, *plus* a $1,676,000 (taxable equivalent) death benefit. This would then position you to have a possible retirement income of $117,000 per year ($1,676,000 x .07) that is 100 percent guaranteed without considering the cash values or dividends related to the whole life policy! The sweet spot from a positioning standpoint is having a 1:1 ratio of your assets to your permanent death benefit. This is how you prevent a pay cut in your golden years!

Returning to the plane analogy where the objective is to land safely at your destination, if you want to land safely with your money in retirement, then your financial decisions need to be integrated and coordinated to achieve maximum benefits and outputs today and in the future. Just like the pilot who performs a preflight check before takeoff and then closely monitors in-flight progress to ensure a safe flight, this same attention to detail should be given to your personal finances.

Chapter 7

IS YOUR RETIREMENT INCOME A SURE THING?

• • •

When it comes to retirement income, there are only two kinds of income: guaranteed or not guaranteed. It is really that simple. Yet, these income options are rarely discussed. If they are, it is usually at the end of a dentist's career when the options for securing maximum income are more limited. Dentists must figure out what portion of their retirement income they want guaranteed. Some dentists want a guarantee on 100 percent of their income. Others say, "I really do not need that much guaranteed, but I would like a portion guaranteed to cover my monthly expenses." In the end, it is a personal decision. However, many of the dentists we work with like the idea of a guaranteed basic income.

Mart

Our objective for our dental clients is to position them to receive a full income replacement at retirement, with as much as 100 percent of that income guaranteed. That is the gold standard! If we plan for the gold standard of full income replacement at retirement, then our dental clients can determine the level of guarantees they would like on their retirement income. Since there are so many unknowns in retirement, the question you always have to ask yourself is: How much of a sure thing do I want? Everybody is different, but when you sit down with clients and discuss the potential roadblocks to enjoying retirement—long-term-care stay, other medical issues, unexpected family needs, and market fluctuations, to name a few—most decide they would like to have at least a portion, if not a significant portion, of their income guaranteed. They understand that when their money is guaranteed in retirement, it becomes a sure thing instead of just a maybe.

• • • • • • • • • • • • • • • • • •

If dentists can go into retirement knowing that their basic monthly expenses are fully covered by guaranteed income sources, then they can have tremendous peace of mind regardless of fluctuations in the stock market or interest rates. It also gives them permission to still invest in the market if they choose to do so with their remaining assets.

Why would a client not want guaranteed income? It comes down to the presence of the rainmakers and the tremendous misinformation that is presented to dental professionals. Types of guaranteed retirement income are, basically, limited to Social Security, pensions, and annuities. If the system is not changed by 2034, a 21 percent reduction in benefits will be necessary to sustain the program.[21] Knowing this, Social Security may not be as guaranteed in the future as it has been for so many up to this point. Also, pensions, such as cash balance plans, are not a viable option for guaranteed income in the dental world, as very few dentists actually have one. That leaves annuities as a form of guaranteed income in retirement.

Annuities can be complicated and confusing. There are many investment advisors, financial planners, and accountants who say you should not have an annuity under any circumstances. Ken Fisher, one of the biggest money managers in the country, markets with a passion against annuities, using the word *hate* in regard to them. This is nothing more than marketing. There is absolutely nothing to hate about a guarantee. As we have said throughout this book, there is no magic financial product. When you look behind the curtain of advisors who are telling you that they hate a product, you can be certain you will find they have an agenda to sell you something else.

In the simplest sense, an annuity is a financial contract issued by an insurance company that provides a series of guaranteed payments to the owner. These payments can be received for a specified period of time or over the lifetime of one or more individuals. Annuities do exactly what corporate pensions do for eligible employees. Purchasing an annuity can be likened to creating a self-made pension:

---

21   Jeanne Sahadi, "Social Security must reduce benefits in 2034 if reforms aren't made," CNN, June 5, 2018, https://www.cnn.com/2018/06/05/politics/social-security-benefit-cuts/index.html.

An individual trades some assets for a stream of guaranteed income. An annuity is a great tool for those looking for secure sources of income in retirement. Unfortunately, when other advisors discourage annuities, this only creates confusion. The response from the client becomes, "Oh, I don't want that."

For most dentists, it is not that they do not want guaranteed income in retirement (because practically everyone *does*). A TIAA-CREF study reported in 2016 that 73 percent of those surveyed wanted to secure their retirement nest egg.[22] We feel that many people choose not to put money into an annuity because they do not understand it. Many are led to believe that money placed into an annuity is forever lost at death. With proper strategies in place, however, this does not have to be the case.

One of the reasons that annuities have received such a bad name is that they have been used improperly for many years. They have been pitched as an accumulation tool by financial institutions and that is not what they were designed for. Annuities were designed as a distribution tool. This is a big difference! Any time you try and use something in a manner other than what it was designed for, it is going to be inefficient. It would be like using a slow-speed handpiece to cut a preparation for a filling knowing that a high-speed handpiece is a more efficient way to get the job done. You wouldn't do it. Buying an annuity for accumulation is the same thing. There are much better ways to accumulate money than purchasing an annuity.

This brings us to one of the main themes of this book: How are your financial assets positioned? As we discussed in chapter 5, the positioning of your assets is key to determining how much income

---

22 "TIAA 2016 Lifetime Income Survey: Executive Summary," TIAA-CREF, September 14, 2016, https://www.tiaa.org/public/pdf/C33638_Lifetime_Income_ExecSummary.pdf.

you will receive in retirement. Making an investment without understanding where the financial asset should be positioned in your overall Financial Treatment Plan will cost you a lot of money today and income in the future. All Americans, including dentists, want the gold standard of achieving a full income replacement at retirement. That is our objective for our clients.

As discussed in the last chapter, the largest retirement income stream is achieved by using a protected asset strategy. This strategy requires that permanent whole life insurance be part of the Financial Treatment Plan. Ideally, you would want to have a 1:1 ratio of your total assets to your whole life death benefit (taxable equivalent) at retirement.

For example, if you have $2,000,000 between your retirement plan and outside investments, then the whole life insurance death benefit on a tax-equivalent basis should equal $2,000,000. In today's interest rate environment, a protected asset strategy in this situation would generate approximately $140,000 at a 7 percent pay-out rate of annual guaranteed income over a lifetime. Upon death, the taxable equivalent death benefit of $2,000,000 or more is paid out to the named beneficiaries (e.g., spouse, children, charities) to fully replace the assets that were spent down in retirement.

The protected asset strategy is possible when the dentist owns whole life insurance and purchases a SPIA with a single life option using retirement funds or other invested assets at retirement. The drawback to a SPIA with a single life option, however, is that this income stops the day you die. Upon your death, any money left in the annuity goes to the insurance company. Although this option will provide the highest income while you are alive, if you do not live very long, the insurance company wins big at this game. Also, if legacy is a priority for you and your spouse, then whole life insurance must be a part of your Financial Treatment Plan in order to elect this income option at retirement.

Although a protected asset strategy provides the highest level of guaranteed income for a retiree, not everyone will pursue this option for various reasons. Nonetheless, if dentists still like the idea of having some guaranteed income in retirement, then they can consider either a SPIA with a joint life rider or a basic annuity with an income rider. Each of these options will provide a reduced level of guaranteed income based on the same $2,000,000 of assets used in the example above. Depending on the dentists' personal situation, one of these options may be the right fit. One thing is certain, if whole life insurance is not part of a dentist's Financial Treatment Plan, the dentist will take a pay cut in retirement. Please refer to table 7.1 that summarizes the various income options in retirement based on having $2,000,000 of assets.

INCOME PRODUCT / STRATEGY	DISTRIBUTION RATE	INCOME GUARAN-TEED?	INCOME PROVIDED FROM $2M OF ASSETS	LEGACY PROVIDED FOR
Protected asset strategy	7%	Yes	$140,000	Yes
SIPA, joint life	5.75%	Yes	$115,000	No
Annuity with income rider	4.5%	Yes	$90,000	Maybe
"Safe" with-drawal or Monte Carlo distribution	3%	No	$60,000	Maybe

Table 7.1

The next retirement option to provide guaranteed income at retirement is a joint SPIA. The income provided by a joint SPIA is payable over two lifetimes (typically, the lifetimes of a husband and wife) and will be less than the income paid under an SPIA with a single life option. If a husband and wife are both sixty-five years of age, the distribution rate today is 5.75 percent. Using the same $2,000,000 of retirement assets, a joint SPIA would provide $115,000 of guaranteed income today. This income will stop at the death of the second covered person. If there is any money left in the annuity, the remaining amount will revert back to the insurance company.

Dentists are enticed when they initially look at these first two guaranteed income options because either one will give them the highest income when looking at multiple choices. But upon further analysis, they realize that if they were to die early in retirement, these options could possibly disinherit their loved ones and the charities to which they hope to contribute. Legacy is provided for a spouse with a joint SPIA option. However, if the dentist and spouse also want to provide for children or charities, then when an SPIA option is elected, whole life insurance should also be adopted as a protected asset strategy in the Financial Treatment Plan. If legacy for children or charities is not a concern, then permanent life insurance is not required.

The final guaranteed income option that we will discuss is an annuity with an income rider. This annuity option is similar to the first two options discussed in that it can produce a guaranteed income over one or two lifetimes. However, it is unique in that if you die with assets still left in the annuity, the remainder goes to your named beneficiaries and not the insurance company. Due to this unique benefit, the income rider on the annuity will offer a reduced distribution rate on the assets placed in the annuity. Today, that guaranteed distribution rate is approximately 4.5 percent for a sixty-five-year-old. Using our previous example of having $2,000,000 of assets at retirement, this will result in $90,000 of guaranteed income each year. In summary, this annuity option will provide guaranteed income for a dentist in retirement without the dentist losing control of assets in the annuity, but at a reduced distribution rate. As we always say, every financial product has advantages and disadvantages.

• • • • • • • • • • • • • • • • • • •

Tim

The income options we just discussed use annuity products to provide effective distribution or income strategies with guarantees at retirement. This is the primary strength of an annuity product and why we refer to them as wealth distribution tools. Unfortunately, just as a lot of things in the world of traditional finance do, products oftentimes end up being promoted as the end-all solution for all financial issues. As we said earlier in this book, there is no such thing as a magical financial product that solves all financial issues.

Despite this, the financial world often promotes the use of an annuity as a wealth accumulation tool by hyping the perceived benefits of a variable or fixed equity-indexed annuity. Benefits often pitched are tax deferral for after-tax assets invested, protection against market losses, suit protection, and a death benefit, to name a few. The question to always ask when making a financial decision is, At what cost am I getting these benefits?

Possible disadvantages to consider when purchasing an annuity for wealth accumulation *only* are the loss of capital gains tax treatment for after-tax assets invested, back-end load surrender charges of up to ten years, and a 10 percent early withdrawal penalty from the IRS on taxable funds withdrawn prior to age fifty-nine and a half. Other disadvantages include limited investment options and, in the case of an indexed annuity, potential earnings lost in a rising market due to low caps or high interest rate spreads. This is why some pundits say they hate annuities.

To reiterate, if accumulation is your sole objective, there are more effective products than variable and equity-indexed annuities. If, however, you are interested "in the rest of the story," as Paul Harvey used to say in his daily radio commentaries, there is no better product than a correctly used annuity when it comes to wealth distribution or guaranteed income replacement.

• • • • • • • • • • • • • • • • • •

Most dentists who desire a guaranteed income source in retirement will select one or a combination of the three annuity distribution options discussed. In addition, depending on their legacy concerns, they may also incorporate a protected asset strategy into their Financial Treatment Plan. If they choose not to go down one of these paths, then, by default, they will accept a retirement income that has no guarantees to support it. This means adopting a controlled, spend-down strategy—spending down principal and interest over a specified period of time—or taking a Monte Carlo safe-withdrawal distribution. Neither option provides a guarantee of success and both can be easily sidetracked in a down market.

In a controlled, spend-down strategy, dentists make assumptions about 1) the rate of return they expect to earn on their retirement assets, and 2) the length of time they want those assets to last. Again, let's assume that a dentist has $2,000,000 in retirement assets at age sixty-five, which he will invest in a conservative portfolio at 3.5 percent. His time horizon for this money would be twenty-five years, or age ninety. Based on the assumptions given above, he would then withdraw principal and interest of approximately $117,000 each year from retirement assets until it was spent down to zero at age ninety. Now, many of you may already recognize the glaring problem with this strategy: if it works as planned and the dentist lives beyond age ninety, he may be out of money. Worse yet, he could run out of money before age ninety if he happens to retire in a down market. Either way, if the dentist outlives his money, not only has he lost his income but there will also be no legacy for his spouse, children, or charities.

In summary, a controlled, spend-down strategy is never one that you would use with 100 percent of your retirement assets. With that being said, it could be effective for a portion of your retirement asset balance in combination with other retirement income strategies.

The last retirement income option we will discuss is the widely accepted and promoted Monte Carlo safe-withdrawal distribution from retirement assets. In this strategy, dentists leave their retirement assets fully invested and hope to maintain, or even grow, their retirement asset base while pulling out a safe withdrawal to live on in retirement. This withdrawal, which may be inflation adjusted, is made each year regardless of whether or not the retirement portfolio had an investment gain or loss. The idea behind this strategy is that in the long haul, dentists can take out income each year without depleting their retirement assets and still leave a legacy to loved ones or charities when they die.

From a historical perspective, a safe withdrawal strategy works most of the time, as confirmed by any number of Monte Carlo simulation calculators available on the internet. A great internet calculator that supports this statement is Vanguard's Retirement Nest Egg Calculator. The one big issue with this strategy, however, is that in order to have a 98 percent likelihood of not running out of money in thirty years, the safe withdrawal rate for dentists can be no more than 3 percent of their retirement assets. Using our previous example of having $2,000,000 of assets at retirement, this would result in a retirement income of only $60,000 annually, none of which would be guaranteed. Even if a 3 percent safe withdrawal strategy could ensure that dentists would not run out of money in retirement 100 percent of the time, it would be unacceptable, due to the low income allowed. Therefore, a safe withdrawal strategy is very inefficient for a retiree.

• • • • • • • • • • • • • • • • • • •

Tim

Throughout our many years in private practice, Mart and I have seen, many times, other advisors recommending a safe withdrawal rate of 4 percent and even higher. Historically, as verified by Vanguard's internet Retirement Nest Egg Calculator, this withdrawal rate of 4 percent is successful only 91 percent of the time over a thirty-year period, based on a portfolio consisting of 50 percent stocks and 50 percent bonds. From another perspective, this means that dentists and their spouses would have a one out of ten chance of running out of money during a thirty-year retirement period. Going back to our earlier airplane analogy, if you knew that you had a 10 percent chance of not landing safely at your destination, would you get on that plane? If the answer is no, then why would you take this same chance in retirement?

● ● ● ● ● ● ● ● ● ● ● ● ● ● ● ● ● ● ●

Many traditional advisors who do not like annuities often recommend some form of a safe withdrawal strategy to provide dentists an income in retirement. They may also recommend other investment strategies to provide the same retirement income. They present their plans by saying, "You can structure your stocks to live off dividend income," or "You can ladder your CDs," or "You can live off your bond interest," to name a few. That is how they sculpt their plans for their clients, but none of these investment strategies are guaranteed. These plans for retirement income are based on a hope and a prayer. If inflation and interest rates are running high, then these eroding factors can devastate a fixed income portfolio. This is the most common option that we see offered by traditional planners, and it provides the least income with greater risk and no guarantees. In baseball, that is a strikeout!

The other thing that comes into play is that the compensation of most advisors in the traditional financial world is based on assets under their management. For some, giving up control of those assets by placing them into an annuity may mean they will give up future compensation from those assets. The business of a stockbroker or investment advisor is focused on maintaining control over a client's assets and managing them, on a fee basis, for twenty to twenty-five years. This underlying objective can prevent advisors from supporting an annuity, a financial strategy that would give their clients increased income and real guarantees in their retirement. Since so few stock brokers and advisors are fiduciaries—who are required by law to do what is in the best interest of their clients—there is little incentive for the stock broker or advisor to expand their clients' knowledge base, which may include recommending an annuity. This is one reason why the government has become involved, from a regulatory perspective, to promote the fiduciary standard.

Mart

As a sidebar, only 10 percent of financial advisors in America are fiduciaries, which is shocking. The other 90 percent of advisors are not held to the same standards. Another name for an investment fiduciary is a registered investment advisor (RIA). We, as doctors, have a fiduciary standard to do what is right for the patient, so why don't we have the same expectations of our advisors? In his book *Unshakeable*, Tony Robbins warns that if your advisor is not an RIA, "Smile sweetly and say goodbye." Tony asks, "Why would you ever choose a financial advisor who doesn't have to act in your best interests over one who does? You wouldn't!" Yet many dentists still work with advisors who are not fiduciaries. We agree with Tony that it is very important to work only with fiduciaries when making financial decisions.

Oftentimes, a major reason dentists do not choose a SPIA with either a single or joint lifetime income option is that they are afraid they will disinherit their loved ones. All legacy concerns are addressed, however, with the ownership of whole life insurance as part of an individual's Financial Treatment Plan. The inclusion of whole life insurance gives you permission to take a higher income in retirement. You can spend and enjoy the assets you worked so hard for all your life and enjoy life to its fullest in retirement. You will have guarantees and peace of mind, knowing that when you die, your life insurance is positioned to fully replace the assets you have spent, whether for your spouse, your kids, or your favorite charity. In baseball, that is a home run!

Successful Financial Treatment Plans are built on strategy, not on products. Even if we found our clients the ideal investment product that delivered a 10 percent rate of return every year, and our clients put all of their money into that investment, they would still lose. Why? Because it is very inefficient to build an exit strategy with only one product. It is almost like a one-person band versus an orchestra. An orchestra with many musicians is going to create more beautiful music than one person playing an instrument alone. In the financial world, when you have a balanced and diversified Financial Treatment Plan, you will have many more options and flexibility to deal with what you face today and in the future. Again, it is not about getting the biggest rate of return. Many times, a moderate rate of return with more benefits is a better option than the home-run investment with a higher rate of return and more risk.

● ● ● ● ● ● ● ● ● ● ● ● ● ● ● ● ●

Tim

Another important issue to understand is that having a strategy alone is not enough. The financial institutions, media, and advisors all promote many different financial strategies that they claim will ensure financial success. Oftentimes, upon full analysis in the Financial Treatment Plan, these same strategies make no economic sense. There are a number of strategies that are totally inefficient from a wealth-building standpoint. They include the strategy to buy term insurance and invest the difference and the strategy to continually compound interest. Both are very inefficient strategies that we see many dentists employing in their financial lives, thinking they are doing the right thing. Instead, they are going in the wrong direction or simply treading water. It is not about *what* product you own but, rather, *how* that product is used in your Financial Treatment Plan that, ultimately, determines financial success.

● ● ● ● ● ● ● ● ● ● ● ● ● ● ● ● ●

In conclusion, we want to circle back to the importance of not taking a pay cut in retirement. Also, do you want a retirement income that is guarantee based through actuarial science or probability based through investments and Monte Carlo simulations? How much of a sure thing do you want? If you wait until you are sixty or older to answer these questions, you will have a more difficult time creating a viable retirement income picture because your options will be more limited due to a lack of time. Possible income guarantees also get watered down when dentists are late to the game in planning for their retirement. When planning for retirement, don't delay! Get started now. *It is what makes your golden years golden!*

Chapter 8

MAKING YOUR GOLDEN YEARS GOLDEN

• • •

Don't let making a living prevent you from making a life.

—JOHN WOODEN

While dentists are hardworking individuals, the fact that they are busy should not get in the way of their creating a life of significance. Throughout this book we have emphasized the importance of having a holistic Financial Treatment Plan. We have also shared some major strategies for income replacement in retirement, but the most powerful strategy involves giving money away to charity. Most dentists are aware of the concept of giving or tithing and the significant impact it can have on our communities, our faith, and society as a whole. Traditional financial planning, however, rarely includes charity in the planning process. Surprisingly, with the proper strategy, giving to charity can mean that you will have more money than if you do not give. That bears repeating, if you do not give, you will have less! It sounds counterintuitive, but as we have said previously, it is not the financial product, but the strategy behind the product that makes you successful. Including charity in your personal plan is a must and here's why.

Dentists want to be charitable, but they are hesitant. Many fear that if they are charitable, they may not have enough money for themselves or they may reduce their family's inheritance. While charity is important to most dentists, they hold reservations about giving.

The reason charitable giving is one of the most powerful distribution strategies is because it is the ultimate triple win. We call it this because if dentists choose to be charitable, they can position themselves to 1) have more income in retirement, 2) avoid disinheriting a spouse or children, and 3) make a gift to the charity of their choice while they live. In this way, everybody wins and nobody loses, a triple win.

Now many of you are probably thinking, how is it possible to increase wealth by giving it away? After all, this is counterintuitive to what we know and understand. In the traditional world, we know that when a check is written to charity, a tax deduction is received. However, the donor's overall wealth is also reduced by the amount of the gift. This is a basic and limited charitable strategy that involves one move of money and creates one benefit: a tax deduction. A triple-win charitable strategy is only achieved once the second, third, and sometimes a fourth move of the money are coordinated with the initial gift. When this occurs, additional benefits of tax savings, increased income, additional wealth, and the preservation of a legacy are possible.

Let's analyze a simple strategy we call turbotithe and compare it to traditional giving. Charities, including churches, schools, and other organizations are always looking for donations. These donations are most commonly made in the form of a cash payment via a check. A direct cash donation to a charity is a very inefficient way to give, even though it may be the easiest. With this in mind, let's compare a direct cash donation (Dentist A) to giving away an appreciated asset under a turbotithe strategy (Dentist B).

It is not unusual for a dentist to own a stock, bond, or mutual fund that has appreciated. When this investment is eventually sold, a capital gains tax of up to 23.8 percent (federal only) will be due upon sale. Wouldn't it be great if the capital gains tax on the sale of this investment could be eliminated? Absolutely!

For this example, let's assume that both dentists have $10,000 in cash and own $10,000 in ABC stock with a cost basis of $5,000. Both dentists believe that the ABC stock is a good one and want to continue owning the stock going forward.

DENTIST A

Dentist A simply writes a $10,000 check to his charity of choice and retains ownership of the ABC stock that currently has an embedded $5,000 capital gain. If Dentist A elects to sell his ABC stock in the future, and assuming the present market value of the stock remains unchanged, Dentist A will then recognize the $5,000 capital gain and pay a $1,190 capital gains tax ($5,000 x .238).

The result: Dentist A gave $10,000 to charity and pays $1,190 of capital gains taxes upon the sale of the ABC stock.

DENTIST B

Dentist B, on the other hand, donates the ABC stock, worth $10,000, to the charity. This means there is *no* tax on the gain from appreciated assets. At the same time, Dentist B takes her cash of $10,000 to purchase $10,000 of ABC stock or some other investment if she wants to rebalance her investment portfolio. The bottom line is that

Dentist B still owns ABC stock (or a different investment), but it now has a new cost basis of $10,000.

The result: Dentist B gave $10,000 to charity and reestablished the cost basis of the ABC stock (or new investment) at $10,000. By handling the donation in this manner, Dentist B eliminated the current capital gains tax of $1,190 on the original ABC stock and still owns the stock.

To summarize, the turbotithe strategy eliminates the capital gains tax on the appreciated asset *and* increases the cost basis of the retained investment holding by repurchasing the stock or new investment. It's a win-win strategy for the charity and the dentist. Without exception, *everyone* who writes a check to charity should consider this strategy. It is not always possible to do so, however, without a having a well-balanced plan.

The turbotithe strategy is excellent for smaller donations. When larger donations are considered for charity, more sophisticated and powerful strategies are available. These strategies often include advanced charitable planning tools, such as a charitable remainder annuity trust (CRAT) or a charitable remainder unitrust (CRUT). Do *not* attempt to implement these strategies on your own. At the very least, your accountant/CPA, and other outside planning experts (e.g., attorneys, professional personnel from charitable foundations) should be involved. You must comply with all IRS regulations if you want a good result with a charitable planning strategy.

Mart

Considering an advanced charitable planning strategy requires going back to what Tim and I have preached throughout this entire book: you must have a properly balanced Financial Treatment Plan. If the bulk of your assets at retirement are held only in a retirement plan, you will be severely limited in your charitable planning options. The type of advanced strategies we're discussing here are much more effective, and you will have more options if you have diversification in your asset holdings. In other words, besides a retirement plan, you will want to own other after-tax outside investments such as stocks, bonds, mutual funds, and real estate. Charitable planning strategies are enhanced even more if these outside investments have appreciated and have long-term gains built into their market value. The long-term capital gains tax on these assets can be completely eliminated with a charitable planning strategy while increasing your retirement income at the same time. This is why financial success comes from diversifying all your assets and not just owning stocks and bonds held inside a retirement plan.

In working with our dental clients, we want to know how they are wired. What are their passions in life? What is close to their heart, whether it be their church, synagogue, alma mater, or other charitable institutions that they may have worked with over the years. If they have a charitable intent, we plant a seed early in the planning process, letting the client know that there could be some very effective charitable strategies in their future. The beauty of these strategies is that you can experience a triple win by having more income in retirement, leaving a larger legacy to loved ones, and contributing to a charity of your choice all because you chose to be charitable while alive.

Regarding the last point, some recognition definitely goes along with making a donation to charity while you are alive. Many people place charitable organizations in their estate plan so that the charity benefits from their donation when they die, but that means they never get to see the results of their gift.

If you had your choice, wouldn't you rather make a gift to charity while you are still alive? Your gift may actually be the one that spurs others to do the exact same thing. The bottom line is that you feel great about helping a charity that is near and dear to your heart, and you get to witness the results.

When a triple-win charitable planning strategy is fully analyzed, it becomes apparent that those who choose not to give will actually be worse off than if they did.

Let's use some real numbers and examine a situation in which a charitable trust is used as part of a dentist's overall retirement planning. As we go through this example, it is important to note that the assets mentioned in this example do not represent the dentist's entire asset base at retirement. In other words, the dentist will have more assets that are held in some type of retirement plan (e.g., IRA, 401(k)) as well as additional after-tax assets.

In this example, we are looking at Dentist A and his spouse, who are both age sixty-five. The combined federal, state, and local tax rates for income and capital gains are 40 percent and 20 percent, respectively. In addition, Dentist A has $150,000 in a retirement plan and $1,000,000 of after-tax assets at retirement (see Figure 8.1). In the traditional world of finance, Dentist A would be looking at an annual income of $34,500, based on a 3 percent safe withdrawal strategy. This is a situation we see all the time.

TRADITIONAL INCOME PLAN AT 65

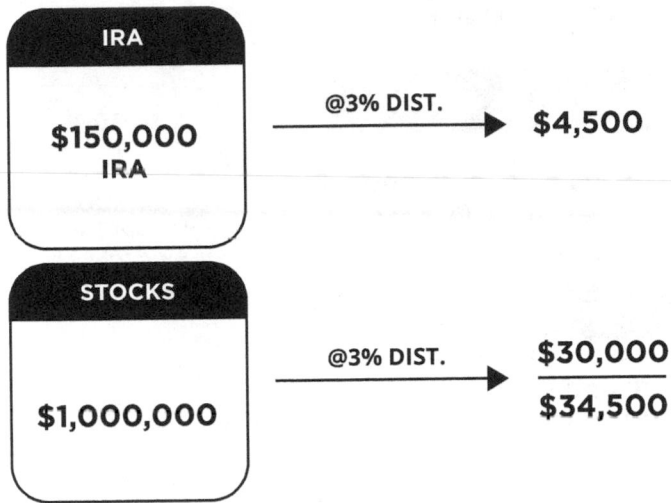

ASSUMPTIONS
MARGINAL TAX BRACKET: 40% F,S,L
CAPITAL GAINS RATE: 20% F,S,L

Figure 8.1

Now using the same facts from above, let's examine a charitable planning strategy for Dentist A and his spouse. This scenario allows the couple to make a sizable charitable contribution and increase their retirement income at the same time (see Figure 8.2). This strategy will require several moves in order to maximize its effect.

CHARITABLE GIVING STRATEGY

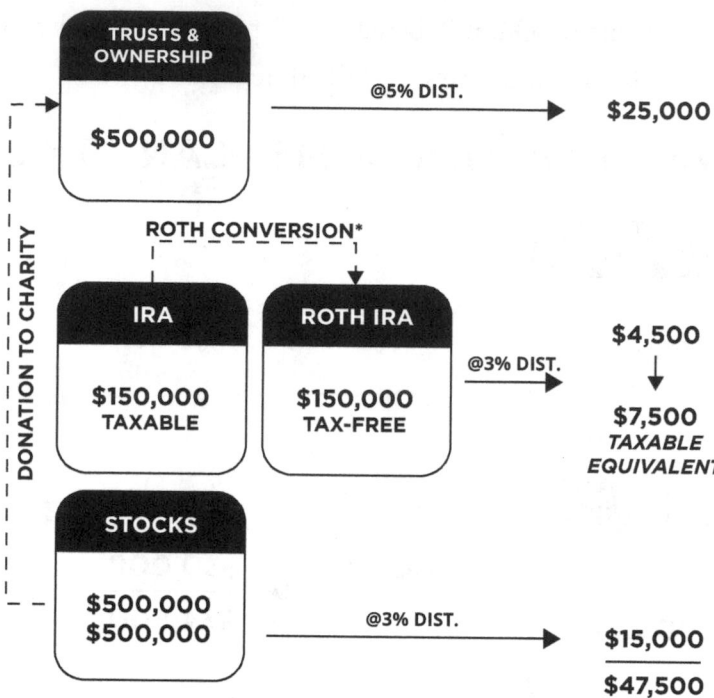

* THE TAXES OF $60,000 DUE ON THE ROTH CONVERSION ARE FULLY OFFSET BY THE TAX BENEFIT CREATED THROUGH THE CHARITABLE DONATION.

Figure 8.2

The first move in this strategy requires Dentist A to gift $500,000 of his after-tax assets to a charitable remainder annuity trust (CRAT) that benefits his charity or charities of choice. Dentist A and his spouse are now the income beneficiaries of the trust. In this situation, Dentist A established the trust to provide a fixed 5 percent distribution (based on the original gift amount) or $25,000 each year. Upon the death of the second spouse, any remainder in the trust will pass on to the charity.

Due to the charitable contribution, Dentist A will receive a charitable tax deduction for that year of approximately $150,000. Because the $500,000 gift is a future gift and not an immediate gift to the charity, Dentist A will receive a discounted tax deduction based on the anticipated future value of the ultimate charitable gift. Based on the facts of this example, the tax deduction will approximate 30 percent of the original gift amount or $150,000. In a 40 percent income tax bracket, this will result in a tax savings to Dentist A of $60,000 for that year. For many, this is the point where their charitable strategy ends. In our example, however, Dentist A is going to take this charitable strategy to the next level by achieving even more benefits.

Dentist A enjoys a second use, or move, by using the tax savings created from the charitable contribution to offset the additional income taxes generated when he converts his IRA to a Roth IRA. In a 40 percent income tax bracket, the $150,000 Roth conversion will generate an additional $60,000 of income taxes. Since the charitable gift was made in the year that the Roth conversion was completed, Dentist A has, essentially, completed the Roth conversion with zero tax consequences. Dentist A now has his retirement money in a Roth IRA, which will provide tax-free income distributions going forward. Assuming a 3 percent safe withdrawal distribution, the Roth will provide him an additional $4,500 of tax-free income during retirement. In a 40 percent income tax bracket, this is equivalent to $7,500 ($4,500/.60) of taxable income.

The last piece of this strategy is the annual income provided to Dentist A from the remaining $500,000 of after-tax assets. Again, assuming a 3 percent safe withdrawal distribution, these assets will provide another $15,000 of annual income to Dentist A.

The total taxable equivalent income provided to Dentist A and his spouse under this ultimate charitable planning strategy is $47,500 ($25,000 + $7,500 + $15,000). This represents an additional $13,000 ($47,500 - $34,500) of annual income for Dentist A, who chooses to be charitable.

In summary, if Dentist A elects to use an ultimate charitable planning strategy based on the facts in this example, he will achieve a double win by increasing his retirement income by $13,000, or 38 percent, plus he will provide a gift to a charity. The third leg of the triple win, which is maintaining or increasing his legacy for his loved ones, should already be in place if Dentist A owns whole life insurance as part of his existing Financial Treatment Plan. If this is not the case, and legacy is important to Dentist A and his spouse, then an additional move can be incorporated into the charitable strategy to acquire whole life insurance.

So why don't all dentists do this? One reason is they don't know about it; no one has ever talked to them about how to accomplish a charitable gift with a win-win-win strategy. Charitable donations have always been thought of as a transaction wherein individuals make a gift to charity for which they receive a charitable tax deduction, but nothing else. This is microeconomic thinking!

Another reason that charitable strategies are rarely used in planning is that the idea or concept was not introduced early enough in the dentist's career. Ideally, you want to have these strategies on the radar, if not already positioned, anywhere from five to fifteen years before retirement. This time frame allows dentists time to position their assets in their Financial Treatment Plans in order to take full advantage of this planning strategy. It still works when you are older. However, it may be a bit more challenging, and you may only get a double win versus a triple win when being charitable.

Mart

The use of a charitable strategy in combination with a traditional retirement plan (401(k), or IRA) can allow dentists to receive a tax deduction upfront on their contribution, a tax deferral on all growth inside the plan, and, finally, tax-free access to their investments at the end. Dentists can only receive all three of these tax benefits through the strategic positioning of assets within the Financial Treatment Plan. Without strategic planning, they will, at most, only receive two of the three tax benefits as highlighted in the following table.

	TRADI-TIONAL 401(K)	ROTH 401(K)	OUR CHARI-TABLE PLAN
Tax-deductible on contribution	YES	NO	YES
Tax-deferred on accumulation	YES	YES	YES
Tax-free on distribution	NO	YES	YES

Table 8.1

It all comes down to building options. The better you are positioned, the more options you will have in the future. Good positioning gives you the freedom to make proactive decisions with your money. It also allows you to be the person you want to be, by giving you the opportunity to be charitable. Finally, giving while you are still alive is much more rewarding than having the donation distributed upon your death. In the end, contributing to a charity is the most powerful distribution strategy, so consider giving more.

Note: The example presented in the above charitable planning strategy is for discussion and informational purposes only. Do not rely on this for accuracy, as you must first consult your own attorney and other professional advisors to determine what may be best for your individual needs.

THE FINANCIAL ENJOYMENT FACTOR

• • •

"The journey to financial freedom starts the MINUTE you decide you were destined for prosperity, not scarcity—for abundance, not lack. Isn't there always been a part of you that has known that? Can you see yourself living a bounteous life—a life of 'more than enough'? It only takes a MINUTE to decide. Decide now."

—MARK VICTOR HANSEN, BEST-SELLING AUTHOR

This book started with a fight for your money, but it is ending with the enjoyment of your money! Its purpose is to introduce information that offers you the opportunity to avoid taking a pay cut in retirement, and at the same time build guarantees into your retirement income. This is the Holy Grail of retirement income planning, but it cannot be attained in the traditional financial planning model. This information is so atypical to what people are spoon-fed by the financial institutions and media that you must have an open mind to accept it. After all, having more income in retirement with guarantees offers you the opportunity to enjoy your retirement on many levels. It also means you get to do what you want without any reservations!

In order to achieve the above objectives, you will need to change your traditional, microeconomic mind-set—one that is often taken in retirement planning—to a more holistic, macroeconomic view. The strategies presented in this book embody a significant paradigm shift from the traditional way of doing things. The traditional world of financial planning is primarily focused on accumulating assets with minimal to no consideration given to the distribution phase. Also, let's not forget about the rainmakers: the government, financial institutions, and corporations. Each of these institutions is in an ongoing battle with individuals for control over their money. Hopefully it is clear to you now how important it is to never relinquish control of your assets.

Planning for the end of your dental career is much more than just accumulating assets. Sure you want to have a big pile of assets, but you want to do it in the most efficient way possible. This means that, throughout your career, you want to build in distribution or exit strategies that will allow you to fully enjoy—both today as well as in the future—what you have worked so hard for.

Our goal is for you to have full income replacement when you stop working rather than taking a pay cut in retirement, as most dentists do. Why take a pay cut when you don't have to? Why not position yourself to fully enjoy life in your retirement and still have enough money to leave the legacy you desire to your loved ones?

Dentists seemingly accept a 50 percent reduction in income upon retirement because that is what everyone else is doing. It's like watching lemmings going over a cliff one by one. Taking a pay cut in retirement is unacceptable. In order to avoid this, you will have to embrace the fact that you cannot accumulate enough assets over your working career to fully replace your income in retirement.

The rainmakers' success comes from understanding the velocity of money and not from accumulating assets. We want you to become the rainmaker of your own success. Instead of succumbing to the rainmakers' recommendations, you need to start thinking as they do. Learning how to multiply your money using the velocity of money principle will change your financial life. You need to be open-minded so that you are ready to take action. Changing your path from a traditional financial path to a holistic, evidence-based Financial Treatment Plan may feel foreign to you at first, but it is the path that will lead to 100 percent income replacement in retirement.

In order to change your financial path, the first step is to change the way you think about money. Think about what you *want* in life, not what you *need*. Unfortunately, traditional advisors focus on needs and goals, as does Suze Orman, "the personal financial guru," who proudly states that she is "the queen of needs versus wants." Needs are weak. In reality, all we really need are food, water, oxygen, and shelter. Goals are also somewhat weak because they are limited to the established goal. Wants and desires are powerful and limitless! Dentists do not come up short in retirement because they don't make enough money during their careers. They take a pay cut in retirement because they have fallen prey to the weak and inefficient strategies promoted by financial institutions, the media, and financial entertainers.

The second step to changing your financial path is to recognize who the rainmakers are and start acting as they do instead of being their victim. There are published books and even a commercial that talk about quantifying a number, the amount of money you may need at retirement. That is an exercise in futility! If you are forty years old today, how do you determine that number when your retirement is twenty to twenty-five years down the road? You don't know what inflation will be over that time. Will your family situation be different in the future from what it is today? What will your experience be in the stock market? Will interest rates change dramatically? How about tax rates? Do you think they may be different from what they are today? Yet, you are being asked to identify a number for a future retirement that may be twenty-five years away. Why not just make the decision that you are going to plan for a maximum income in retirement, and whatever that maximum amount is, that is the best you can do. We guarantee that a maximum amount will be a whole lot better than your perceived need, number, or goal is today.

We call this reaching your maximum financial potential. Just as athletes strive to reach their maximum athletic potential, we want you to meet your maximum financial potential. Unfortunately, you can never do that if you live in a needs-based world. It is impossible! Instead, focus on your wants and build your Financial Treatment Plan with those desires as the foundation. What do you want? Identify your wants and desires first if you want to live a happy and successful life.

Step three to changing your financial path is to know that you need a macroadvisor. You will not be able to reach your true, maximum financial potential without having a skilled advisor to lead and direct a team of advisors who will engage you throughout your lifetime. There may be dentists who accumulate a lot of assets, but they do so at the expense of having no exit strategy in place. As a result, they will get minimum enjoyment from their money in retirement. They will also be exposed to all kinds of risks, which may cause their money to disappear overnight because they don't have guarantees built into their financial plans. The do-it-yourselfers will never achieve their maximum financial potential.

As a dentist, if you have a cavity, are you going to stand in front of a mirror, drill that cavity out, and fill it yourself? Not a chance. You will go to a colleague and have that professional do the dental work. In the same vein, why wouldn't you want professionals on your team, helping you become financially successful? The answer for most is that an advisor burned them in the past, or they witnessed their parents' self-made financial success. For some, their ego gets in the way of accepting advice.

Do-it-yourselfers are the most limited when it comes to financial planning because they do not engage any advisors. As a result, they unknowingly place themselves behind the eight ball. They are penny wise and pound foolish because they think they are saving on fees and commissions. In the end, however, they are going to be very disappointed with their results. Trying to be a Lone Ranger with your personal finances will sabotage your financial future. We all need a Tonto by our side!

Then there are dentists who engage a traditional advisor who is only focused on helping clients accumulate wealth or build the biggest pile of assets. Again, we also want to accumulate maximum wealth, but if it is done at the expense of building effective wealth distribution and conservation strategies in the Financial Treatment Plan, you will lose. Traditional advisors live in the world of accumulation and linear thinking. Their focus is on accumulating assets in a retirement plan. Also, they usually only recommend term insurance to cover their clients' life insurance needs. As we discussed earlier in this book, if you enter retirement without owning at least some whole life insurance in your Financial Treatment Plan, you will take a pay cut in retirement.

The traditional path of financial planning is very inefficient and is directly responsible for the plight of most dentists today, who are retiring on roughly 50 percent of their preretirement income. These are your fifty-percenters! Remember the 50 percent analogy at the beginning of this book? It is a failing grade. Unfortunately, it is far too common to see dentists, today, who are in their fifties and wondering why they are not further ahead financially. Worse yet, they know in their gut that they are headed for a huge pay cut in retirement.

Change is difficult, and changing the way you think about your money can make you extremely uncomfortable. Money is a very emotional topic, and when the decision comes down to emotional or financial reality solutions, emotions will, unfortunately, win in most people's lives most times. A general rule to consider is that we all tend to gravitate toward the path of least resistance. In the world of personal finance, this means that decisions are often made based on what everyone else is doing. If this is an effective way to make financial decisions, then why are so many dentists struggling financially today?

Too often, dentists just stay with their plan to avoid the discomfort of change, but this decision comes with a significant loss of wealth and life-enjoyment today and in the future. Hopefully, we have presented in this book the reasons that will spur you to consider, and ultimately commit to, making that change!

* * * * * * * * * * * * * * * * *

Mart

Years ago, before I met Tim, I attended a financial seminar during my residency in Michigan. The person leading the seminar had a certificate that I had to sign at the end of the meeting. It was my promise that I was going to make a change in my financial life.

For whatever reason, signing that certificate made me feel good. Prior to this meeting, I had never really been exposed to or taught about personal finances. I can remember thinking, as I signed that certificate, that I was going to commit to learning more about how money worked and how I could best make money work for me and my family. That was the start of my lifelong journey of learning about financial information. The signing of that certificate taught me one of the most important things in life, which is commitment. I invite you now to make that same commitment to learning more about your personal finances and how you, too, can reach your maximum financial potential.

• • • • • • • • • • • • • • • • • • •

We have no problem saying that you should not have read this book if you cannot make a change. Unless you are committed to take action, reading the advice in this book is, quite frankly, a waste of your time. Talk and information are cheap without action and implementation. To produce the results we have discussed in this book, the commitment from you must be there, but that change may be uncomfortable at times. Hopefully we have provided you with a deeper understanding of the implications of not changing. Most people cannot afford the consequences of inaction.

If you are thirty-five years old, you may think that you have plenty of time to get your personal finances in order before you retire. The fact is those years are going to pass more quickly than you can imagine. Before you know it, you will be staring retirement in the face.

Instead of letting time pass, why not use it to your advantage? In order to best use the time, you must change how you think. You cannot take action on these principles and strategies until you open your mind.

A first step to opening your mind is to ask each of your advisors to verify and support every recommendation they make when it comes to your finances. As we have explained throughout this book, every financial decision will have an output, benefits, and, most importantly, costs associated with it. You should expect a full account of all three of these factors before committing to any financial decision. Also, is each financial decision in your Financial Treatment Plan coordinated and integrated with all others? In other words, is there a synergy between your financial decisions that is moving you forward financially, or are they stalled or even moving you backward? If you do nothing else, you should at least learn to expect a full account of the output, benefits, and costs of your financial decisions. As Ronald Reagan once said, "Trust, but verify, watch closely, and don't be afraid of what you see!"

The ultimate objective of this book is to open your mind to the very real possibility that you can fully replace your income in retirement with guarantees and still have the opportunity to donate to charity without reservation—in other words, to live life on your terms. This is the enjoyment factor.

If this is of interest to you, and you want to learn more about how to change your mind-set to achieve the perfect smile in retirement with a Financial Treatment Plan that demands pay-cut prevention for your golden years, please contact us at our website: yourretirementsmile.com, or call us at 1-800-281-0703. We are also happy to answer your questions at info@macro-wealth.com.

Finally, for those of you who are curious about your retirement readiness, please take our assessment at **www.yourretirementsmile. com** to see how close *you* are to retiring without taking a pay cut in your golden years.

Acknowledgments

There are a number of people we would like to acknowledge for their part in making this book possible. It is safe to say, however, that if it were not for Robert Castiglione and his passion for finding, explaining, and verifying the truth when it comes to financial decision making, we would not be putting these words to print. He invented and developed the system we use today. The power of this process is that it has stood the test of time over many decades and many different economic environments without having to change to accommodate the whims of the market or the economy. We are not aware of any other financial system that can do this.

Bob's ability to challenge the status quo and not accept the misinformation that is so prevalent in the financial planning world has helped thousands, and likely millions, of people across America reach their maximum financial potential. We are blessed to know Bob as a friend and to have his wisdom cross our paths years ago.

If it were not for Bob and his system, Tim would have washed out of the financial services world, as have so many other advisors searching for the truth. In March 1994, when Tim first saw this financial process for creating wealth, he knew within fifteen minutes that he had finally found what he was so desperately seeking for his clients. If Tim had not discovered this process, Mart would not have experienced this system and learned how it could benefit his family and the dental community.

We would like to recognize all our clients, who, after experiencing this process, say, "Why haven't I heard this before," or "It sounds like a no-brainer to me!" or "This makes so much sense." Dentists who are open minded and motivated to make a change embrace this system very quickly and appreciate the verification process behind it. Also, those dentists who engage in this process are significantly financially ahead of their peers and colleagues who continue to do what is recommended in traditional financial circles.

In addition, we would like to thank our mentors and friends who have further helped in shaping who we are and what we do. Without a strong network of mentors for lifelong learning, which includes people such as Al Dickens, Mike Welker, Lucian Ioja, Gabor Nagy, Mike Steranka, Brian Gengler, Art Sanger, John Smallwood, Pat Sweeny, Dave Connelly, and many others, we would not be the advisors that we are today!

Finally, and most importantly, we would also like to thank our spouses, Julie and Lindsey, for their unconditional love and support as we travel across the country lecturing, attending meetings, or holding evening webinar meetings with clients. Their support and understanding has made it possible for us to help as many people as we have. As Warren Buffet once said, "The difference between a golden egg and a goose egg in retirement is the chick you marry!" There is a lot of truth to that statement!

In closing, successful people realize that they need to surround themselves with people who help to advance their lives, from spouses, to friends, to team members, mentors, and business colleagues. We are THANKFUL and GRATEFUL that these people have helped us in more ways than we can put into words. Please, from the bottom of our hearts, enjoy our book!

About Macro Wealth Management

Dr. Mart McClellan and Tim Streid are presidents of Macro Wealth Management. The firm's niche is the dental and medical professions. Both Mart and Tim are registered investment advisors and each brings a unique perspective to their practice. Mart is still practicing as an orthodontist, and Tim has a strong professional background as a CPA. Their knowledge and experience creates a lot of trust with the clients they serve all over the United States.

Mart and Tim utilize an economically based financial model to create short- and long-term financial strategies for dentists. The foundation of their success is the use of a macroeconomic strategy that is based on economic principles and not opinions. Macro Wealth Management is the only dental-focused financial firm in the country that uses this model. Mart and Tim have lectured nationally and internationally to large and small groups. They welcome future opportunities to speak with groups of any size.

TIM STREID

Tim entered the wealth management business in 1989. By the end of 1993, Tim was disillusioned and considering a new career path, like many individuals who pursue a career in financial services. Tim was disillusioned and considering a new career path. Tim had been trained, as an auditor, to look at a company's entire set of books before signing off on an opinion. Because of this, he was frustrated when he entered the traditional world of finance and found that it did not embrace this same approach when helping clients to make life-changing financial decisions.

Instead, Tim was asking clients to make financial decisions based mostly on sales hype and opinion (as promoted by the financial institutions) rather than informing them about a comprehensive process that allowed them to discover and verify the best financial decisions for their personal situations. Tim knew there had to be a better way. Fortunately, in March 1994, Tim was introduced to the planning system and process that he still uses to this day. This planning process changed his life, and more importantly, the financial lives of his many clients. Throughout his career, Tim has continued to develop and hone a business philosophy that approaches wealth management from a unique, holistic perspective.

Tim serves as president of Macro Wealth Management and is a registered investment advisor. He graduated from Eastern Illinois University in 1984 and began his career working as a CPA with the big-four public accounting firm of Peat Marwick. Tim has spoken on personal finance at numerous speaking events all over the United States.

Tim resides in Peoria, Illinois, with his wife, Julie. They have three children: Taylor, Mark, and Grant. They have been actively involved in their children's athletic activities over the years and have officially joined the ranks of empty nesters now that their youngest son, Grant, has entered college.

In addition to his passion for his family and helping others achieve financial success, Tim also lends his time to improving his community. He is active in several organizations as well as his church. Tim is also an avid golfer and enjoys the lake life with his family.

MART MCCLELLAN

Mart McClellan brings a unique perspective to the financial advisory profession because he is not only a financial advisor but also a practicing orthodontist. Mart received his dental degree from Northwestern University and completed his orthodontic residency at the University of Michigan. His undergraduate degree was procured at DePauw University, where he discovered dentistry while on mission trips to Kenya and Guatemala.

After having a number of financial advisors, he was referred to Tim by a fellow dental school classmate. Tim introduced Mart to the unique, holistic model that they use to this day. The model worked so well for Mart and his family that he wanted to disseminate this information to other health professionals, knowing firsthand that this information was not taught in dental school. As a result, Tim and Mart formed a partnership in 2004 and started Macro Wealth Management.

Mart is also president of Macro Wealth Management, a registered investment advisor (RIA), and registered in multiple states in the financial fields of securities, life and disability insurance, and annuities.

Mart lives in Lake Forest, Illinois, with his wife, Lindsey. They have two children, Riese and Flynn, and a big dog named Bruno.

CPSIA information can be obtained
at www.ICGtesting.com
Printed in the USA
FSHW010711291119
64570FS